". . . Gary Soto's writing style can't be easily explained by a label. It has the heat of afternoon sidewalks and the spring of well-worn tennis shoes. For the hungry reader, tired of arid stretches of the bestseller lists, *A Summer Life* is like a ripe, cool peach snatched from a neighbor's tree."

—*Metro*, San Jose, California

". . . delicately expresses those moments we sometimes forget for years, then return to unexpectedly . . . appraises human conduct with compassion and tender irony . . . concentrating on his characters' attitudes to only the most important human questions: love, growing up, the passing of time, fear, death."

—*San Francisco Chronicle*

Gary Soto has written six poetry collections, prose recollections, and several books of essays. His first young adult short story collection, *Baseball in April and Other Stories*, has been one of the most widely discussed and reviewed books of 1990. He is Associate Professor of Chicano Studies and English at the University of California, Berkeley.

GARY SOTO

A Summer Life

Published by
Dell Publishing
a division of
Bantam Doubleday Dell Publishing Group, Inc.
666 Fifth Avenue
New York, New York 10103

For my brother Rick

The trademark Laurel-Leaf Library® is registered in the
U.S. Patent and Trademark Office.

The trademark Dell® is registered in the U.S. Patent and
Trademark Office.

ISBN: 0-440-21024-0

RL: 6.2

Reprinted by arrangement with University Press of New
England

Printed in the United States of America

September 1991

10 9 8 7 6 5 4 3 2 1

RAD

CONTENTS

ACKNOWLEDGMENTS

"The Locket," "The Bike," "The Inner Tube," "The Haircut," "The Taps," "The Weather," "The Hero," and "The Computer Date" appeared in *This World* of the *San Francisco Chronicle*. "The Drive-In Movies" appeared in *The California Monthly*. "The Buddha" appeared in *The Threepenny Review*. "The Fights," "The Hand Brake," "The Guardian Angel," and "The Catfish" appeared in *Puerto del Sol*.

The author wishes to thank Jose Novoa for helping shape this book, and the editors of these magazines, especially Lyle York.

PART ONE

THE BUDDHA

I killed ants here, and pulled puncture vine there. *There* was a small rise of earth and oily weeds at the junkyard at Van Ness and Braly. At the young age of five, I couldn't go far, maybe to the side of the house where I looked down the long throat of the alley, to Mr. Drake's palm tree where pigeons warbled at the top of a leafy world, or to the front steps where I played with the ceramic Buddha my uncle had brought back from the war. The Buddha was happiness, a great smile and large belly, soft colors, and a robe splotched with gold. He usually rested on the small table near the telephone and rattled when the phone rang. The Buddha was the most beautiful thing in our house, that and a Japanese garden sculpted in a seashell. When my mother was away, I took the Buddha out to the front steps and played a game in which he "Ho-Hoed" a belly laugh and walked on lines of ants.

On a day when I knew my mother was going to be gone a long time and my sister fell asleep from the heat, I carried the Buddha to Van Ness Avenue. I held him up and said, "We can't go over there." Van Ness was a busy street, bluish with diesels and large sedans, yellow with an occasional taxi. Buddha smiled, and I rubbed his belly. I pressed my thumb on his gold splotches. I listened to a diesel downshifting, the grind of gears hurting the air. I sat the Buddha in the dusty weeds and killed red ants with my thumb.

I collected shards of broken glass lit with sunlight. I searched for wire, loops of bright copper that my uncle said were worth money. I worked my fingers into the asphalt to pull out a bottle cap. I couldn't read so I sniffed the cap. I thought I would smell root beer or 7-Up. I smelled the odor of metal, which lingered in my nose all day. I scraped the cork from the metal cap, and it came out in flakes.

Diesels turned slowly onto Braly Street, their shadows square and full of dust, their gears grinding dry-toothed, their heavy brakes sighing. They were heading toward Sun Maid Raisin, where our family worked behind a penitentiary of tall windows. The diesels were moving so slow that I thought I could try to run through the space between the front and back wheels.

I stood on the dirt curb, panting. I looked at the Buddha, half-hidden in weeds. His smile was dark and his belly busy with red ants exploring his roundness. I saw a diesel crawling slowly up Van Ness, large but not scary enough for second thoughts. When it entered Braly, I ran to its side, then drifted left until I was under it and looking up, my head just a few inches from the undercarriage, my legs pumping as fast as they could go. I gritted my teeth and told myself, Hurry! Hurry! After twenty steps I drifted out from under the truck, and skidded in the dust. I waved to the driver, whose face I could see in the mirror, but I didn't see him return my wave. Black smoke coughed from the truck's tall pipe, and its gears ground into third.

I returned home with the Buddha, set him near the telephone and wiped his face free of dust while my sister cried in her crib. Mother came home carrying bags of plums and peaches that my sister and I ate on the steps. Later, we went to my grandmother's cellar and watched Uncle Junior cut balsa wood into parts for his glider.

The cellar was lit by one bulb. Dusty jars of nopales lined one wall. I sniffed the air. Although the scent of bottle cap was still in my nose, I picked up a dank smell, a ghost of cool air blowing from under the house. I liked the smell, and liked my uncle when he said I could have the scraps. I made a tiny plane and later crashed it a hundred times until only slivers remained.

When Uncle Junior's collie got hit on Van Ness, I watched him pant on the side of the road, his eyes quiet with the dusk that had captured the street. I couldn't see what was wrong with the dog. No blood flowed, no tears streamed, no protruding bone made the dog curl his lips. He just seemed tired, and Uncle seemed tired as he lifted him into his arms and told us kids to get the hell away. He started up the alley, with pain in his arms.

The air was cool but the asphalt hot. I walked in

a small circle looking for the bottle cap. I stood in
the weeds and said to myself that there was where
the Buddha had been. But I didn't know this place.
The grass had sprung back where the Buddha had
rested, and it was too dark to slash a stick across
the hole where ants came and went with crumbs
of the living in their great little jaws.

THE GRANDFATHER

Grandfather believed a well-rooted tree was the
color of money. His money he kept hidden behind
portraits of sons and daughters or taped behind
the calendar of an Aztec warrior. He tucked it into
the sofa, his shoes and slippers, and into the tight-
lipped pockets of his suits. He kept it in his soft
brown wallet that was machine tooled with
"MEXICO" and a campesino and donkey climbing a hill. He had climbed, too, out of Mexico,
settled in Fresno and worked thirty years at Sun
Maid Raisin, first as a packer and later, when he
was old, as a watchman with a large clock on his
belt.

After work, he sat in the backyard under the
arbor, watching the water gurgle in the rose
bushes that ran along the fence. A lemon tree
hovered over the clothesline. Two orange trees
stood near the alley. His favorite tree, the avocado,

which had started in a jam jar from a seed and three toothpicks lanced in its sides, rarely bore fruit. He said it was the wind's fault, and the mayor's, who allowed office buildings so high that the haze of pollen from the countryside could never find its way into the city. He sulked about this. He said that in Mexico buildings only grew so tall. You could see the moon at night, and the stars were clear points all the way to the horizon. And wind reached all the way from the sea, which was blue and clean, unlike the oily water sloshing against a San Francisco pier.

During its early years, I could leap over that tree, kick my bicycling legs over the top branch and scream my fool head off because I thought for sure I was flying. I ate fruit to keep my strength up, fuzzy peaches and branch-scuffed plums cooled in the refrigerator. From the kitchen chair he brought out in the evening, Grandpa would scold, "Hijo, what's the matta with you? You gonna break it."

By the third year, the tree was as tall as I, its branches casting a meager shadow on the ground. I sat beneath the shade, scratching words in the hard dirt with a stick. I had learned "Nile" in summer school and a dirty word from my brother who wore granny sunglasses. The red ants tumbled into my letters, and I buried them, knowing that they would dig themselves back into fresh air.

A tree was money. If a lemon cost seven cents at Hanoian's Market, then Grandfather saved fistfuls of change and more because in winter the branches of his lemon tree hung heavy yellow fruit. And winter brought oranges, juicy and large as softballs. Apricots he got by the bagfuls from a son, who himself was wise for planting young. Peaches he got from a neighbor, who worked the night shift at Sun Maid Raisin. The chile plants, which also saved him from giving up his hot, sweaty quarters, were propped up with sticks to support an abundance of red fruit.

But his favorite tree was the avocado because it offered hope and the promise of more years. After work, Grandpa sat in the backyard, shirtless, tired of flagging trucks loaded with crates of raisins, and sipped glasses of ice water. His yard was neat: five trees, seven rose bushes, whose fruit were the red and white flowers he floated in bowls, and a statue of St. Francis that stood in a circle of crushed rocks, arms spread out to welcome hungry sparrows.

After ten years, the first avocado hung on a branch, but the meat was flecked with black, an omen, Grandfather thought, a warning to keep an eye on the living. Five years later, another avocado hung on a branch, larger than the first and edible when crushed with a fork into a heated tortilla. Grandfather sprinkled it with salt and laced it with a river of chile.

"It's good," he said, and let me taste.

I took a big bite, waved a hand over my tongue, and ran for the garden hose gurgling in the rose bushes. I drank long and deep, and later ate the smile from an ice cold watermelon.

Birds nested in the tree, quarreling jays with liquid eyes and cool, pulsating throats. Wasps wove a horn-shaped hive one year, but we smoked them away with swords of rolled up newspapers lit with matches. By then, the tree was tall enough for me to climb to look into the neighbor's yard. But by then I was too old for that kind of thing and went about with my brother, hair slicked back and our shades dark as oil.

After twenty years, the tree began to bear. Although Grandfather complained about how much he lost because pollen never reached the poor part of town, because at the market he had to haggle over the price of avocados, he loved that tree. It grew, as did his family, and when he died, all his sons standing on each other's shoulders, oldest to youngest, could not reach the highest branches. The wind could move the branches, but the trunk, thicker than any waist, hugged the ground.

THE TAPS

Not much happened when I set a rock on the railroad tracks. I expected a great noise of iron and pig squeals and an avalanche of lumber. I expected the conductor to hold onto his engineer's cap and sparks to bloom as the train slid on its side. I expected steam and hot, devilish coals bouncing down the street, setting fire to the broom factory, which in turn would set fire to the L & R Book Company. The flames would march from factory to warehouse, and in no time all of Fresno would be on fire.

We *were* on fire. The July heat was a blond locust with square jaws feeding in the trees. The asphalt was a soft, blackish river on which cars traveled, windows down, the passengers soaked in sweat. Dogs whined, even in the shade of toolsheds, and my *abuela*, tired of watching me circle on her small brick patio, said for me to go play somewhere else. I had just hammered taps to the bottoms of my shoes and liked hearing their tinny music.

I was happy to leave the brick patio. I figured I could hear my taps better on a cement sidewalk. I walked up the alley, crossed the street and stood in the sun, a mustache of sweat dripping around my mouth. Mother had warned us not to cross the street. She warned us not to do a lot of things, like eat raw bacon at the Molinas, like climb hand over hand on telephone lines, like play with matches in the weeds where our father poured used motor oil. But we weren't very good listeners. Now that I had crossed the street, I was scared of a spanking, but not scared enough to turn back. I looked down at my shoes, black puddles of leather, and stomped one heel gently. I loved the sound of taps, the way the little clinks made me feel grown up. I took one step, then another, left over right, right over left as I skipped and imagined sparks flying out from under my shoes. I watched my shoes intently, head down, and in no time I was lost. I turned around, hot in the face. I could see the Sun Maid Raisin Tower and Mr. Drake's palm tree, and had a feeling that my house was where the sycamore scared up wild branches.

I looked down at my shoes, then shaded my eyes. A block away, train tracks wavered in the heat. I hurried over, less in tune with the music of my taps than with the long rip of the train whistle. A passenger train the color of spoons rushed by. I was disappointed because I wanted to wave to the engineer. I was also disappointed for not thinking quicker about hanging onto the gate as it rose straight as a sentry.

A man the color of a sparrow walked near the tracks. I thought about waving and saying, "The train will be here," but he was dirty, and his mouth was blistered. The soles of his shoes were tied with twine. His coat was ripped like a sail. I remembered Mother's warnings about poor men who lived near the train tracks and knew enough not to bother him.

I played with the gravel as I waited for the next train. I pulled at foxtails and pounded a bottle cap with my fist into the soft asphalt. I smelled the inside of a Cracker Jacks box, crushed flat by a car tire. I stirred an ant hill with a splintered plastic spoon and collected the shark teeth of broken bottles. When I heard the far away sound of a train, I wiped my hands on my pants, set a rock on the tracks, and enjoyed wild thoughts about the train overturning. As the train rumbled closer, a plume of black smoke riding over its back, I felt a rumbling in my chest. The wind stirred dust and litter of candy wrappers and milk cartons. The sparrows on the shiny rails took flight. The gate lowered and a bell clanged to the beat of the red signal.

I hid behind a spidery tumbleweed as the train grew closer, its hypnotic eye of light swirling in its socket. The train was huge and black, and for the first time since my brother and I had tried to burn down our house, I felt something really exciting was going to happen. I held my breath, hands over my ears, as the train met up with its fate, *me.* But I stood up from behind the tumbleweed, again disappointed, when the rock just ricocheted off the tracks. Car after car swaggered past and the man in the caboose just stared when I waved.

I managed to return home by keeping an eye on the Sun Maid Raisin tower. I snatched three plums from a Japanese family's yard and watched the Molinas hammer roller skates to the bottom of a rickety dog house. At home, I washed my face with a garden hose and rested in the shade of our almond tree, petting my dusty shoes with wet Kleenex. I waited for dinner and nightfall, when in the dark I could race around *abuela*'s patio, whistling like a train and kicking up the engine of sparks that lived beneath my soles.

THE HAND BRAKE

One afternoon in July, I invented a brake for a child's running legs. It was an old bicycle hand brake, which I wore on a belt loop, the cable tied around my waist, and whose function was to help me stop when I came racing to the end of the street. I found it in the alley that ran alongside our house, among rain-swollen magazines, pencils, a gutted clock, and sun-baked rubber bands that cracked when I bunched them around my fingers.

I couldn't read or write, or tell time without thinking that the long hand made the hours go by too fast. But I put the rubber bands to good use immediately by letting them fly at a sauntering cat. The cat, its face like a three-cornered hat, hurried away, keeping its tail up.

The hand brake was made of chrome that hurt my eyes when the sun lit its edges. I sat on the magazines, mesmerized because every time I pinched the lever of the hand brake, the cable moved, not unlike when I pulled on a tendon of a chicken claw, and its filthy toes clenched.

I walked home slowly and met up with the cat, who now crouched in the stench of weeds where motor oil was poured, its eyes large with worry because he sensed something was up. My brother was eating a watery peach and blowing on his palm.

"What's that?" my brother Rick asked, a bib of peach juice on his shirt.

"Thing from a bike."

My brother showed me his palm, where a sliver had gone in quick as a stitch on a sewing machine when he climbed the rabbit hutch at the Molinas' house. I winced and asked if it hurt. He squeezed it until a bubble, clear as glass, popped from the wound.

I polished the hand brake with the same liquid Mom used to clean the floor and spent the afternoon pulling the lever until I was bored and thirsty for something to do. I got it into my head that I should wrap the cable around my waist and think of the lever as the thing that made me stop and go. It was mostly go for a five-year-old running up and down the block, the sun yellow, tree-high and slanting over the junkyard.

My brother, two years older, wiser from glass-punctured feet, nose bleeds, and now a sliver in his palm, didn't think much of this game. He watched me from the shaded porch where flies circled, a halo of black around his head, and called me stupid for staying in the sun. But nickel-colored water from the garden hose cooled my head, and yellow-green apricots from a low branch where sparrows flittered watered my tongue.

Mr. Drake, our neighbor who had given up chasing his chickens, drank water from a hose and yelled at me to sit down because he was getting hot just watching me. "Your mother is going to find you dead," he said. "It's not right to run out there." *There* was the street, soft asphalt that we sometimes pulled up in little chunks because someone said it was good to chew.

I looked at the sun's sparkling edges, and spiders dropping eggs on dry skeins. I listened to Mr. Drake, who wagged a wrench-thick finger at me, and sat under the chinaberry, where I ate a plum and fondled the lung-shaped leaves of bean plants. I liked how they felt, soft and cool, and liked how they drank squirts of water from a Coke bottle.

Then I raced down to the railroad tracks on Van Ness. The sun gleamed off the steel rails. The wind moved a hat-sized tumbleweed, and I raced after it. I raced a taxi filled with sailors, and danced from one foot to the other foot when the crossing guard dropped and the red light and iron bell began to throb. The train, huge as a cloud, beat me by inches to the wind-whipped oleander that I had picked as the finish line.

When I returned home, I was dusty from my naked feet to the crystals of dirt on my eyelashes. I drank water from the garden hose and cooled myself with six plums. I was tired but happy.

I rose to my feet and went to my *abuela*'s to run with her three chickens. When the cat came out of the weeds, shaking a lanyard of long grass from her paw, I tightened the hand brake and came to a stop. The cat stopped and looked at me for the longest time, knowing from this and previous lives that he should stay away from half-naked kids. He hurried away, ears pulled back, and I hurried after it, the cable jumping on my waist, the lever shining with sunlight and God's forgiving stare.

THE GIANT

My brother measured the length of the cement shoe prints with his hand. For all we knew, they were set before our grandmother came from Mexico to this country, which to us made them as old as the very dirt in our garden. Summer brought buttfaced plums, hours in the shade, and an itch to ignore Mother's warning about what lay at the end of the street, where we discovered a broom factory, rows of trucks loaded with blocks of hay, and a crazy neighbor who held a live chicken in her arms as she rocked on the porch, a tin can of drool at her feet. We looked and ran, nearly tripping over the broken sidewalk around a scabbed sycamore.

The length of the shoe print was almost three of my brother's hands, and four of mine. We rose to our feet, knees creased with grass, and eyed each other, then followed the shadow of a rumbling moving van downshifting to a stop. We were amazed and couldn't hide our excitement when later, over dinner, we told Father, his shoulders giving off the fragrance of sawdust from his new job as a carpenter, that a giant lived nearby and we had better keep our eyes open if we didn't want to get squashed. Father didn't stop chewing to ask questions, or let our warning worry his brow. Mother, sweater over her shoulders, looked out the window, where in an hour the summer dusk would settle in the alley. Far away, we heard the sound of the broom factory starting the night shift.

After dinner, we had to sit on the sofa. Mother said we would get sick if we played after we had eaten, and said our meal, a round steak and *frijoles,* was deciding where to latch onto, an anemic arm or a skinned knee. We sat fooling with our fingers and staring at the venetian blinds that banged when a breeze stirred. This was before TV, before long pants and shoes on our feet, before Christ became a glow-in-the-dark statue we kept on a night stand.

I noticed that my fingers were smaller than my brother's, not as dark, and a lot cleaner. Black dwelled beneath his fingernails, and a pink scar ran along his thumb where he got caught on barbed-wire. His breath rattled like a leaf. His neck held a pulsating blue vein as large as our father's. For a moment I thought my brother might become a giant, that it would be only a matter of time before he could fill the window with one scary eye. His naked feet were large, and his head had trouble staying straight up. It seemed to me that it always leaned one way or the other. I thought about this a while, then decided my brother was only a brother, not a giant with crashing feet.

After ten minutes on the sofa, we got up and helped with the dishes by putting away the forks and spoons. Mother handled the water glasses and the plates, which were blue with ancient scenes of Chinese dragons and temples. When she finished, we stood watching the steam rise from the gray, soapy dishwater and thought deeply about the cold pipes that rushed water to us from snow-slushed mountains. We watched the water, mesmerized by the transaction of heat to air, both of us glad that we lived in a house where you could press an ear to the wall and hear the faraway sounds.

With the dishes out of the way, my brother and I scurried down to the end of the block to look once more at the shoe prints, which now seemed smaller, though not small enough to calm our minds. I got down on my knees and measured my hands in the print: three-and-a-half hands, not four. When I lifted my hand, two red ants were pressed into my palm, staggering with bent antennas and broken legs. With a cheek fat with summer air, I blew them off, only a little scared of the red ant's bitter bite. Rick said that a million ants could easily fill those prints, and if the ants decided to do it one day they could flood over to our house when they were through.

Rick and I returned home, darkness gathering around trees, bushes, and parked cars. We played with a punctured, multicolored beach ball under an orange porch light until I stubbed my toe on the cement steps and my sobbing reminded Mother that it was late and we still had to bathe.

We bathed in scalding water and cooled off. In bed, I listened to the broom factory, the loud whack of straw being wired onto red, yellow, and blue sticks. That was another worry, because I had once said hello to a worker, and he had said hello back. One day, he might show me the machinery, and by accident I might fall into a hamper of straw and get tangled in the machine that tied the wire.

I got up and stood at the window, the smell of crushed chinaberry in the warm summer air. The junkyard facing our house was a silhouette of iron pipes and jagged sheet metal. A dog barked as a car circled out of a driveway, the sweep of headlights passing over my hands as they clutched the windowsill. Back in bed, I closed my eyes, convinced that because the giant's brain was so far from his feet, he would have no pity when he turned onto our street.

THE BIKE

My first bike got me nowhere, though the shadow I cast as I pedaled raced along my side. The leaves of bird-filled trees stirred a warm breeze and litter scuttled out of the way. Our orange cats looked on from the fence, their tails up like antennas. I opened my mouth, and wind tickled the back of my throat. When I squinted, I could see past the end of the block. My hair flicked like black fire, and I thought I was pretty cool riding up and down the block, age five, in my brother's hand-me-down shirt.

Going up and down the block was one thing, but taking the first curve, out of sight of Mom and the house, was another. I was scared of riding on Sarah Street. Mom said hungry dogs lived on that street, and red anger lived in their eyes. Their throats were hard with extra bones from biting kids on bikes, she said.

But I took the corner anyway. I didn't believe Mom. Once she had said that pointing at rainbows caused freckles, and after a rain had moved in and drenched the streets, after the sparrows flitted onto the lawn, a rainbow washed over the junkyard and reached the dark barrels of Coleman pickle. I stood at the window, looking out, amazed and devious, with the devilish horns of my butch haircut standing up. From behind the window, I let my finger slowly uncurl like a bean plant rising from earth. I uncurled it, then curled it back and made a fist. I should remember this day, I told myself.

I pedaled my squeaky bike around the curve onto Sarah Street, but returned immediately. I braked and looked back at where I had gone. My face was hot, my hair sweaty, but nothing scary seemed to happen. The street had looked like our street: parked cars, tall trees, a sprinkler hissing on a lawn, and an old woman bending over her garden. I started again, and again I rode the curve, my eyes open as wide as they could go. After a few circle eights I returned to our street. There ain't no dogs, I told myself. I began to think that maybe this was like one of those false rainbow warnings.

I turned my bike around and rode a few times in front of our house, just in case Mom was looking for me. I called out, "Hi Mom. I haven't gone anywhere." I saw her face in the window, curlers piled high, and she waved a dish towel at me. I waved back, and when she disappeared, I again tore my bike around the curve onto Sarah Street. I was free. The wind flicked my hair and cooled my ears. I did figure eights, rode up the curbs and onto lawns, bumped into trees, and rode over a garden hose a hundred times because I liked the way the water sprang up from the sprinkler after the pressure of my tires. I stopped when I saw a kid my age come down a porch. His machinery for getting around was a tricycle. Big baby, I thought, and said, "You can run over my leg with your trike if you want." I laid down on the sidewalk, and the kid, with fingers in his mouth, said, "OK."

He backed up and slowly, like a tank, advanced. I folded my arms behind my head and watched a jay swoop by with what looked like a cracker in its beak, when the tire climbed over my ankle and sparks of pain cut through my skin. I sat up quickly, my eyes flinging tears like a sprinkler.

The boy asked, "Did it hurt?"

"No," I said, almost crying.

The kid could see that it did. He could see my face strain to hold back a sob, two tears dropping like dimes into the dust. He pedaled away on his bucket of bolts and tossed it on his front lawn. He looked back before climbing the stairs and disappeared into the house.

I pulled up my pants leg. My ankle was purple, large and hot, and the skin was flaked like wood shavings. I patted spit onto it and laid back down. I cried because no one was around, the tears stirring up a lather on my dirty face. I rose to my feet and walked around, trying to make the ankle feel better. I got on my bicycle and pedaled mostly with the good leg. The few tears still on my eyelashes evaporated as I rode. I realized I would live. I did nothing fancy on the way home, no figure eights, no wiggling of the handlebars, no hands in my pockets, no closed eye moments.

Then the sudden bark of a dog scared me, and my pants leg fed into the chain, the bike coming to an immediate stop. I tugged at the cuff, gnashed and oil-black, until ripping sounds made me quit trying. I fell to the ground, bike and all, and let the tears lather my face again. I then dragged the bike home with the pants leg in the chain. There was nothing to do except lie in the dirt because Mom saw me round the corner from Sarah Street. I laid down when she came out with the belt, and I didn't blame the dog or that stupid rainbow.

THE ALMONDS

It was early August, and the almonds were bitter, almost not worth cracking with a hammer. They were not worth the fear, either. I had taken my uncle's army belt, the wide one with black eyeholes on which grenades hung (or so he told me), and strapped it around my waist. Once up in the tree I could latch it and my small four-year-old

body onto a sap-sticky limb. I could eat from there,
look around and think of the past, which for me
was a play that had already notched three or four
scars on my imperfect knees.

The furry outer shells I tossed to the weeds, or
our cat, Boots, who sat near the water meter, her
eyes spinning like the dials that registered how
much water we used. The inner shell broke open
with a squeak when the hammer came down.

The first taste was bitter, the second less bitter,
and by the fifth seed, I was liking them enough to
think I could live in a tree and get by until the start
of kindergarten. I ate like a squirrel with a burst of
jaw motion, a quick look around, and more jaw
motion. The wind stirred the leaves and my nostrils filled with the scent of almonds and oily
smoke from the metal works on Van Ness Avenue.

As I ate, I began to think that maybe I liked
almonds better than my favorite fruit, the plum. I
tried to remember the icy cold taste of plums, and
how the juice trickled from my mouth when I bit
too hard. But the plums were gone. All that remained of them were dark splotches on the side of
the house. My brother and I had splattered them
because we were bored and tired of eating them,
because a hive of wasps lived under the eaves, and
we thought we were doing good. But the wasps
didn't leave, and the only thing we got from
Mother was a spanking.

From my position high up in the tree, I looked
into Mr. Drake's yard, where a rooster spent his
day walking in a circle, and Mr. Drake, an old man
shrinking in blue overalls, spent his afternoons

watching the rooster. They blinked alike, their
small liquid eyes responding rapidly when the
wind stirred the eucalyptus. They watched the
mailman trudge up the front steps. They looked
skyward when the shadow of a cloud touched
them. They nearly stopped breathing when an alley cat climbed foolishly into his yard. And they
were both skinny, the rooster from eating dirt and
feathery seeds the trees dropped, Mr. Drake from
living off the whittlings of a check his son sent
monthly.

Mr. Drake didn't like our family. Our water line
was connected to his, and every three months he
stood at his fence, waved the water bill from the
city, and said we drank and flushed our toilet too
often.

"I could hear," he would say. "That toilet of
yours keeps me awake."

"Your chicken keeps me awake," my mother
would argue back. "Why don't you eat it?"

He didn't have a toilet, just a lopsided outhouse,
the weathered boards warped and slivery, the
hole for fresh air dark as the hole he sat on every
morning. He didn't have much of anything. His
house was as lopsided as his outhouse, the roof a
patchwork of shingles he must have come across in
the alley. His garden was a scraggly vine of worm-
dark tomatoes, and his fruit trees were stunted
and cracked where an awful sap flowed. Not even
weeds entered his yard.

From the almond tree, I saw him watch his
rooster. He sat on a tree trunk, his face pale as
straw behind a straw hat. The rooster strutted in a

dust-stirring circle, occasionally pecking at the ground, now and then running his beak through his feathers.

I hammered another almond, my ninth. I hadn't liked the taste of almonds at first, but the more they became embedded in my back molars, the more I thought my brother would enjoy them too. I thought about other things I had eaten, white cheese for instance, the kind with holes like the holes in my T-shirts. Maybe I was wrong about not liking them and the circles of squash that mother smothered in tomato sauce.

I adjusted myself in Uncle's army belt and heard Mr. Drake turn on his faucet. Nickel-colored water spilled at his feet as he lapped at the end of the hose. I cleared my throat of almonds and ran my tongue over my back molars because I knew it would take a lot of voice to reach our neighbor.

"Mr. Drake," I yelled. "You're spilling the water on the ground!"

Mr. Drake and his rooster looked up, their eyes liquid and small as seeds. He took off his hat, which was frayed with age, and asked, "Who's that?"

"Me, in the tree!"

He squinted into the shaking leaves as I moved to a higher branch. He backhanded the drops of water on his mouth, and asked again, "Who's that?"

"Me, Mr. Drake. I live here."

I dropped the hammer, he dropped the hose, and the scrawny rooster, with a faint heartbeat, ran behind a block of wood.

THE MAGIC TRICKS

My brother pulled a penny from his ear when he was six. I was five and learning to tie my shoes because my mother said it was now or never, seeing that I was finished with an unruly year of kindergarten, where I managed to learn the primary colors but little else. She was tired of me getting my shoelaces caught in the spokes of my tricycle, tired of having to wipe her hands on her apron and trudge down the steps to set me free.

Rick said, "Watch this," and a bottle cap that I recognized from my collection then appeared from his nose. I touched his nose softly, amazed that my brother could do something other than beat me up. When he coughed and a dry apricot rested in his palm, I looked into his mouth. When he scratched his hair and a twig fell out, I smoothed his hair.

"How'd you do that?" I asked. I coughed a dry cough three times but only the sour smell of just-eaten pickles issued from my mouth. I scratched my hair, and an oily film waxed my fingertips.

"Magic," he said and turned away. I followed him as he walked up the alley, begging to know, my shoelaces dragging in the dust, the tongues of my tennis shoes lapping up foxtails and sticker plants.

"Come on, Rick," I begged. "Just teach me the

bottle cap one." He told me to go away, that he and Arnold, a neighbor kid whose arm was palsied from traveling through the washing machine wringer, were going to practice dangerous animal magic. He didn't want me to see. He said it was magic that sometimes leaped back on people, turning them into cats or dogs.

"You're lying," I snickered. I was getting used to my brother tricking me, saying things like, "Captain Kangaroo lives across the street from us"; "Annette Funicello is a fifth-grader at our school"; and "You can die three times before you're really dead."

I returned home to sit in the shade of the back porch with my sister. I practiced loop, bow, tug, but the laces, black from dragging in the dirt, kept getting knotted until they looked like my kindergarten scribbling. My sister Debra, with small fingernail-polished hands, helped me untangle them and wrap the long laces around my naked ankles. I walked around the yard thinking that maybe this was another way of tying shoelaces and perhaps Mother would be satisfied when she came home from work. I had two days to learn or she was going to take away my shoes.

I was feeling good about learning to tie my shoelaces when Rick came back into the yard. He looked at us strangely, his eyes bugged out so the white showed. He said, "A car ran over me and used up one of my lives. I have two more."

"Rick, why don't you cough and show Debra the apricot pit?" I asked. "And you didn't die."

"I did."

"You didn't," I argued, remembering that the man across the street from us was a plumber, not Captain Kangaroo, and Annette Funicello was just a picture cut from a magazine and tacked on the fifth-grade bulletin board.

Rick coughed and a rubber ball rolled from his mouth, the kind used in a game of jacks. He sneezed, and a jack fell from his nose. He rubbed his eyes with his fists, and two marbles gleamed at us.

I turned to Debra. "Magic."

Rick quivered his outstretched fingers at my shoelaces and said, "I predict they'll come untied." I took a few steps and, sure enough, they tumbled from my ankles.

I was proud that my brother knew magic, and trusted him when he said, "Go ahead and burn the house down."

We had started playing with matches, progressing slowly from burning gum wrappers to milk cartons. Bored with these small-time fires, we decided to go all the way now that we had Rick's magic to save us. I stuffed newspapers in the corners of the living room and lit them with a tiny light of a match. We stood back, watching the flames leap waist-high into the air. Debra clapped, and I leaped to the rhythm of the flames. We were so happy that when Rick returned from the sun porch with a crate of cherry tomatoes, I had no qualms about having a war inside the house.

"You missed, Kraut!" I shouted to Rick as I rolled from behind the couch to the stuffed chair. I looked over the chair, dodging the tomato bullets.

Finally, one splattered my T-shirt, and I feigned death, then rose again. "You dirty coward," I screamed. "I have two more lives."

The blood of tomatoes stained the walls, dripping seeds that reminded me of my sister's baby teeth. Pete, our yellow canary, beat his head against the bars of his rusty cage, terrified. The fire burned down to ashes that floated in the air.

We were happily exhausted. Debra fell asleep, and I dozed in the bedroom, only to wake to Rick screaming that it was my fault. Mother was home, and the first thing that leaped to my mind that might save me from the biggest butt-whipping since the beginning of the world, was magic.

I looked in the kitchen, the air still dark with floating ash. I wanted to tell Mom about how Rick could sneeze bottle caps, but decided she wouldn't listen. Snot ran from Rick's nose as he cried. A lump of hair stood up on his head from being yanked. Mom looked with eyes of fire at me, and I said sheepishly, "Mom, I can tie my shoes now."

I hurried to the bedroom for my shoes, sobs choking my throat like a whole loaf of bread. I was wrapping the laces around my ankles when, by magic, I dodged my mother's belt and scrambled out the window, with only one of my lives gone.

THE WAR YEARS

The Korean War was over, and after a year in Japan, our uncle was discharged. He returned with a porcelain Buddha, a tattoo of a blue panther with red claws, and an army blanket for sleeping on our screened porch. In the summer light, flies circled the air, a halo of black, and the water heater popped and rumbled in the corner, where the mop and broom leaned. The neighbor's dog barked behind a slat fence, and chickens screamed as their necks were chopped off next door. In the nearby junkyard, an acetylene torch hissed against pipes and the lava flow of beaded metal. Still, Uncle slept soundly. His face was dark with stubble and moles, creased from a hard sleep. For the first few days his snores were frightening.

By the third day, I was no longer scared of Uncle. I watched him sleep on his small cot, his blanket rumbled like a range of mountains. I pressed my thumb into the eye of the panther tattoo. I ate plums and watched him snore, then open one eye and look at me. He closed his eyes and snored even louder. I put a plum to his mouth, and he took a small bite, chewed but didn't swallow. He then turned over on his back and stretched. I fed him plums until he opened his eyes, got up, and helped himself to coffee.

While Mother and Father worked, Uncle

watched over my brother, sister, and me. He rose late, just before the mailman in his pith helmet leaned his bike against our fence. Uncle drank coffee, sat on the brick steps that faced the Coleman Pickle Company, played cards at the kitchen table while our dime-store parakeet looked on, and went away for hours at a time. Then he would come home and listen to the radio, the venetian blinds filling with wind. The Buddha glowed splotches of sunlight from the window, and the siren at Sun Maid Raisin sent men home from work.

Sometimes he played with us. Debra was always the princess. My brother and I were donkeys braying a set of small, childish teeth. The game was this: Uncle would pretend that the garden hose was off when it was really folded back, squeezed. When we got close, he would squirt us and chase us as far as the spray of water could leap. Rick was older and knew the hose was on. I was young and not too bright. It seemed like it was off, only a few drops dripping from the end of the hose. Therefore, I got my face drenched, my mouth filled, and an ear splashed with cool water. I tripped as I tried to get away and was black with mud by the end of the day.

Sometimes he chased us, and once caught, hung us upside down by our feet from a paint ladder. We laughed, and Debra laughed, too, and did a jig from foot to foot. Once, Grandma spooked me by showing up while I was hanging from the ladder. She looked at me, and asked, "Are you Ricky or Gary?" I answered, "Gary," then tried to explain why I was hanging upside down. She wiped off the giggling drool from my mouth. She went inside our house because she had a bag of lemons, and enough to do during the day without listening to a boy's explanations.

Uncle never spoke of the war. It was 1954. Our street was an industrial street with a few houses, and the diesels that passed our house reminded him of work. His first job back in the States was collecting copper. He said that copper was important during the war. I helped him by learning to tie my laces because I needed shoes where we were going. After his morning plum and coffee, we set out for the alleys, pushing back dusty weeds, searching behind boxes and boards, yanking wire from abandoned cars and trucks. He said it was shiny and reddish-brown, and I thought of the markings on our Buddha when the afternoon sun flooded the living room. With a long fingernail, he stripped a wire of its rubber insulation. "See," he said, "it's like this."

We looked for copper wire until we were out of sight of Sun Maid Raisin and walking, heads down, near the railroad tracks near Van Ness Avenue. Uncle was luckier than me. His hands gripped long and short strands of copper. I carried one strand, a twig of copper worth less than a penny.

By the end of the day, all our copper was worth no more than two dollars. Uncle, now shirtless, drank ice water on the lawn, in the shade of the house. I sucked a plum and ran the hose over my feet. Work was over. Our cat, Boots, dozed in the ferns. Uncle laid down and dozed until he heard a buzzing sound. He sat up quickly and looked sky-ward, eyes squinting. I followed his gaze, but saw only a branch of a brown tree, two flitting birds, and the madness of gnats hovering over the grass. The buzz got closer and closer, until I couldn't hear myself say, "Uncle, what is it?"

Uncle stood up, wiping flakes of grass off his pants, and shaded his eyes. The panther tattoo on his shoulder tightened. The claws dripped red. The noise above was a blimp, white against the summer sky. Uncle followed the blimp to the front of the house. Some of the neighbors came out onto their porches. A car stopped and the driver got out to look. The blimp hovered over Coleman Pickle, then veered left, toward downtown, and became a feathery cloud in the distance. When I asked him if it was anything like war, he said, "No, it's noth-ing like war," then returned to the backyard to nap on the summer grass.

THE SIRENS

The grass around the junkyard was yellow, and the sky was blue above the brick warehouses. I liked the grass and the cough of dust that rose when I ran a hand through it. There, red ants carried white lumber on their backs and a cricket chirped music from its dry thighs. The rocks clacked when struck together and sometimes

threw out sparks. The dragonflies scared me when
I saw them out of the corner of my eye, but I never
saw one touch ground. Since age five when I was
more or less a part of the ground, I figured they
wouldn't bother me. I played in front of the junkyard and looked up now and then at Charlie's Market. People came and went, fumbling for coins in
their pockets. Cars came and went, and diesels
wound down to a near stop as they turned onto
Braly Street.

Mother said that it was OK to play in the grass.
Our house was still in view, and I could see the
ceramic Buddha that I had taken out and left on
the steps. The Buddha smiled as his belly shone. It
was OK to walk up and down the street, from the
end of the junkyard, where I could lean with one
foot on the curb into Van Ness Avenue to the end
of Mr. Drake's house, where I could lean with the
other foot on the curb into Sarah Street. Sarah
Street was mostly houses with dusty shadows,
scraggly limbs of sycamore and elm, and Mr.
Drake raking the same pile of leaves. He was as old
as bark and too cheap to water his yard. His yard
was dust, iron pipes stacked along the fence,
stunted fruit trees and wilted tomato plants, and
boards he sometimes burned to keep warm. His
three chickens pecked the ground for seeds from
the shedding palm and blinked the way rain blinks
when it hits water.

On Van Ness there was plenty to see: train tracks
and trains, diesels, a pickup carrying yellow-white
straw for the broom factory, and men loading and
unloading furniture at Beacon's Storage. There

was also Charlie's Market, where people came and went, munching on pies and sandwiches, and drinking from long, cool bottles. What I ate came mostly from trees, plums being my favorite and plentiful. And grapes, too. I ate them slowly, all the way down to the last sour grape on the naked stem.

Because I was five, what I knew best was at ground level. When a siren first sounded, I looked around and thought it was coming from the junkyard. I looked in and saw pipes for plumbing and sewers, and sheets of aluminum flashing in the sunlight. I looked at Charlie's Market. Workers on their break were looking skyward, hands shading their brows. I followed their gaze. I thought I would see a plane, or maybe a punctured blimp tilted and falling as its air hissed out.

But I couldn't find the source of the noise. The siren wailed awhile longer, then stopped. For a few seconds there was silence. Even the birds on the telephone wire were still. Finally, the workers in front of Charlie's Market turned away. The diesels suddenly seemed not to make any noise at all.

Later, at home, I asked my brother about the noise. He said that it was an air raid siren because a war was going to start. I asked my mother about the war, and she said that there would be one, and our uncle, who was living with us now that he was back from Korea, said that one might come soon. I asked him about the air raid siren, and he said it was to keep us safe.

"Where will the war come from?" I asked. Uncle stood up from his cot, his tattooed shoulders taut with panthers, his ribs filled with shadows. He pointed west, to where I played in the grass in front of the junkyard. He said it wouldn't come from Japan or Korea. Those wars were over. It would come from China, he said, and said that it wouldn't last long.

The next day the air raid siren sounded again while I was in the grass with the ceramic Buddha, doing nothing but watching the cars pass and people eating from wrappers in front of Charlie's Market. I knew something would happen. Fierce heat bounced off sheets of aluminum. Birds with splayed beaks leaped from the wire into the grass, their gray eyes depthless. I touched the Buddha because Uncle said he was a sort of god, and I could understand God because I knew one prayer. I thought I could hide in the grass, but the red ants found me out. When one bit me, I smashed him with my thumb as the sting of tears came to my eyes. But immediately I knew it was wrong. A bomb would be like a thumb, a shadow coming down. I tried to help the ant, but it was severed in two, and only one half was twitching.

The ants were red with anger when the siren started and the workers in front of Charlie's Market stopped their chewing, then chewed again when they thought it was safe.

THE COLORS

Grandfather's favorite color was the green of dollar bills. On summer evenings he watered his lawn, the jet of water cooling his thumb from eight hours of stapling wooden crates at Sun Maid Raisin. He knew that his house, pink as it was, was worth money. He knew that if he kept the rose bushes throwing out buds of sweet flowers, the value of the house would increase. The fruit trees would grow and thicken with branches to feed his family and neighbor.

Grandmother was also fond of green, but preferred the silver shine of coins that made her eyebrows jump up and down. She showed me a nickel slug from the county fair stamped: MILK IS GOOD. She could not read or write in Spanish or English and thought the coin was worth more than a brown child realized. I wanted to say that it was nothing. It could sparkle in the sun or make a nice necklace, but it was no rare coin. I drank my purple Kool-Aid, crunched spines of air trapped in the ice cubes, and made my eyebrows jump up and down like hers.

Yellow was her favorite color. Yellow roses floated in a bowl on the windowsill. The yellow sunshine clock hummed on the wall, and her yellow refrigerator, the first on the block, blended well with the floor, a speckled affair with some

yellow but mostly black. From a top shelf of the
hallway closet, she took down a shoe box of papers,
including a single stock certificate from a sewing
machine company. I looked closely at the yel-
lowed paper and noted "one share" and the date
"1939." It was now 1961, and even though I was
young, nine at the time, I guessed that the stock
was worth the memory of hope but little else.

"When you marry, honey, I will give this to
you," she said, shaking the paper at me. "You'll be
a rich man."

My eyebrows jumped up and down, and I went
outside to the backyard to play with my favorite
color, mud. At my grandparents' house there were
no toys, no pets, no TV in English, so when I stayed
there I had to come up with things to do. I tried
rolling summer-warmed oranges around the yard
in a sort of bowling game in which I tried to knock
over sparrows that had come in search of worms.
But after twenty minutes of this I was bored. I did
chin-ups on the clothesline pole, but that was
sweaty work that bored me even more.

So I fashioned mud into two forts and a great
wall on which I stuck flags of straw-like weeds.
When the mud dried hard as a turtle, I pounded
the hell out of the forts and wall, imagining that a
Chinese war had come. I made bomb sounds and
moaned for the dying. My thumb pressed a red
ant, and I said, "Too bad."

Mud was a good color, and the purple of plums
made my mouth water. Peaches did the same, and
the arbor of greenish grapes that I spied in the
neighbor's yard. Their German Shepherd, ears

erect, spied me too, so I couldn't climb the fence and help myself. But looking was almost like eating, and noon was near.

The brown of *frijoles* was our favorite color as steam wavered in our faces. Grandfather, who came home for lunch, left his shoes near the door, smothered his beans with a river of chile and scooped them with big rips of tortilla. I ate with a fork and a tortilla, savoring little mouthfuls of beans with a trickle of chile. The clear color of water washed it all down, and the striped candy cane left over from Christmas sweetened the day. Grandfather, patting his stomach, smiled at me and turned on the radio to the Spanish station. For dessert, there was dark coffee and a powdered donut on a white plate. Grandmother sipped coffee and tore jelly-red sweetness from a footprint-sized Danish.

While Grandfather played a game of solitaire, I fooled with the toothpicks in the wooden, pig-shaped holder, the only thing that resembled a toy in the house or yard. I swept the crumbs from the table and pinched the donut crumbs from Grandfather's plate. Grandmother did the dishes, ever mindful of the sweep of the sunshine clock. "Viejo," she said, "it's time."

I walked Grandfather to the front yard, where he stopped and said to me, "A pink house is worth lot of money, m'ijo." We both stood admiring the house, trimmed with flowers and a wrought-iron gate, a plastic flamingo standing one-legged in front of a geranium. This was home, the color of his life. We started up the block, me taking two

steps for every one of his, and he said no one's
lawn was as green as his. When we looked back,
when Grandfather said I should go because it was
time to work, Grandmother was at the front window beating the dusty windowsills with a dish
towel, waving goodbye until later.

THE RHINO

I got up quickly on my knees in the back seat of
our Chevy and stared at a charging rhino painted
on the side of a tire company. His legs were
pleated with lines, his horn broken, and his eyes
yellow and furious. I stared at the rhino until my
father's car pulled around the corner, its sluggish
shadow following closely behind, and we flew onto
the freeway.

I looked at Father. His shirt was brilliant white
in the late sun. He was working something from
his teeth with a matchbook cover, and Mother was
penciling words into a black book. I wanted to ask
about the rhino but I knew that they would shush
me.

It scared me to think that tires were being made
from rhinoceros hides. So many things were possi-
ble. We were eating cows, I knew, and drinking
goats milk in cans. Pigs' feet came stuffed into
cloudy jars. Cheese came in blocks from an animal
that ate something very orange or very yellow.

The Molinas stirred bony pigeons in pots of boiling water, and a pig's happy grin showed up on the bacon wrapper. Hopalong Cassidy was a face that appeared on milk cartons, his hand on his pistol, and what I noticed was that his horse didn't have any feet. I imagined that someone had cut off his hooves and the horse had to lay down for the rest of his life.

I knew some of our clothes were cut from hides. Father's belt had an alligator look, his lathering brush was the whiskers of a docile pony, and his shoes, whose tips were mirror-bright, were cowhide. My own shoes were also leather and small as toy trucks. Mother's sweater was wool. Her pillow was a restrained cloud of chicken feathers. Her key chain was a rabbit's foot with a claw that drew blood when raked against skin.

Our neighbor had a bear skin rug spread on his living room floor. Uncle Junior had a shrunken head that swayed from a car mirror. The mouth was stitched closed with black thread and the left eye was half-open. My aunt wore a fox fur with claws clipped together in friendship. The fox's eyes were smoke-brown marbles, but his teeth, jagged as my aunt's, were real. And my cousin Isaac, two years older with kindergarten already behind him, showed me a bloody finger in a gift box. He wiggled the finger and I jumped back, terrified.

I sat back down. I watched mostly the sky, billboards, and telephone poles. A sonic boom scared Mother and had me back on my knees looking around. The sky was pink as a scar in the west where the sun struggled to go down. Birds huddled on a chain link fence, and because I could count to ten I used all my fingers to tell Mother there were eight. Mother looked up from her book, turned on her knees, and ran a comb through my hair.

Father pulled off the freeway, and after two sharp turns, he pulled into my *nina*'s yard, scattering chickens and a large black dog. The dog sniffed us as we got out, and I was so scared that he might bite, Father pulled me into his arms and put me on a low peach tree while he went inside the house. I thought of eating one of the peaches but knew that the fuzz would make my face itchy. I pressed a finger into a brown sap, counted the number of peaches, and peeled bark from the limb. The dog trotted away and the chickens returned to peck at the dust.

That evening we watched boxing. Father drank beer and I sat near him with two links of Tinkertoy. The first television was on, and he and my godfather were watching two boxers hurt each other very badly. They sat at the edge of their chairs, their fists opening and closing. Father had taken off his shirt. Godfather's watch lay on an end table, glowing in the semi-dark of the living room. Both shouted and crushed beer cans when their fighter stumbled into the ropes. I let the Tinkertoys fight each other and grunt like the boxers. I said, "Mine is winning."

Back home I had asked Father if our car tires were made from rhinos, and he laughed. Mother laughed and wiped her hands into a chicken-print

apron. Uncle with his panther tattoo, claws tipped
with blood, pulled on my cheek and said I was
crazy. He assured me tires didn't come from rhino
hides but from rubber that dripped from trees into
buckets. He turned on the porchlight, a feast of
orange light for the moth, and led me down the
brick steps to the Chevy that ticked from a cooling
engine. He pounded a front tire with his fist. I
tried to wiggle free, but his grip held me there. He
made me pound the tire and pet it like an animal.
Black rhino dust came off, dust and fear that I
washed with a white bar of soap when we returned inside.

I was four and already at night thinking of the
past. The cat with a sliver in his eye came and
went. The blimp came and went, and the black
smudge of tire. The rose could hold its fiery petals
only so long, and the three sick pups shivered and
blinked twilight in their eyes. We wet their noses
with water. We pulled muck from the corners of
their eyes. Mother fed them a spoonful of crushed
aspirin, but the next day they rolled over into their
leaf-padded graves.

Now the rhino was dying. We were rolling on his
hide and turning corners so sharply that the shadows mingled with the dust. His horn was gone, his
hooves and whale eyes. He was a tire pumped
with evil air on a road of splattered dogs and cats
and broken pigeons in the grills of long, long cars.

THE SHIRT

Uncle Shorty was back from the Korean War and living in our sunporch, his duffel bag in the corner, his ceramic Buddha laughing on the sill, his army uniform hanging like an invisible man on a hanger. He slept late, and when he woke, he drank water and ate fruit we snatched from the neighbors' trees. Back then there didn't seem to be much. We had sunlight, dogs, a blue-throated parrot, a cat that eventually ate the parrot, an almond tree in the yard, and the daily sounds of our neighbor's motorboat engine puttering alive and churning water in a barrel.

Uncle was home. My brother, sister, and I left him alone because Mom said he was tired, but we, my baby sister first, started piling onto him to wake him up because there was every chance that he would tie us with a length of clothesline and hang us upside down from the ladder leaning against the house. The world was different that way, upside down, my brother or me swinging like sides of beef in a cold-storage locker.

What I liked best about Uncle was his shirt, which was different from mine. My shirt I had to put on, button up, and tuck into my jeans. With a polo shirt like my Uncle Shorty's, you slipped into it and let it go unbuttoned. He sometimes, in a special flip-flap way, tucked his Camel cigarettes into the sleeve. I had a pocket for my things, which were mostly pits of eaten fruit, a broken-toothed comb, some shavings of leaves, and the tiniest of tiny pebbles.

Uncle knew I liked his shirt. I used to slip it on when he was asleep, and at the age of five I knew the smell of a man who went and came back from war. It was more than sweat and beer, tobacco and the splash of cologne. It was the shape of muscle, the anger of a tattoo panther hiding behind cotton, the hair in the collar, the small hole where a bullet could have entered and exited without his dying.

He said he could get me one if I helped him collect copper, which after the war was a precious metal. I started off with him early one morning, he in his polo shirt and I in my button-up shirt of giraffes, elephants, and lions. As we walked up the alley, Uncle jumped at the plums from a neighbor's tree and told me about collecting copper. He said that the metal was shiny, was in the shape of wire, and was often inside machinery.

"Why will someone give us money for it?" I asked. He gave me a second plum and said it was for the war. He asked if I had listened to the sirens, which during the 1950s went on when you were slurping soup and thinking that your life would march on forever. He said that the siren was a warning. He said that even inside the siren there was a bundle of copper wires that sent the electricity from the ground to the throat of the siren.

This was my instruction, two blocks from home, where our neighborhood gave way to diesels, oily railroad tracks, and the horrible slamming of machinery. I gazed at the ground, which I noticed was busy with so many things: the flakes of egg shells, nails, broken bottles, bottle caps pressed into asphalt, grass along fences, sleeping cats, boards, shattered snail shells, liquid-eyed jays, pot holes, black ants, red ants, jaw-lantern insects with blue eyes, half-eaten fruit, ripped shoes, buttons, metal slugs, cracks in the earth, leather thongs, ripped magazines—everything except copper.

The yellow sun was now nickel-colored, hot and vicious on our necks. Uncle managed to gather a few twigs of copper, which he let me hold. When he wasn't looking, I bit back the rubber insulation and saw that the copper was truly shiny, not bitter like a penny but somewhat sweet, like electricity.

We swiped more plums from an abandoned house where Uncle searched the fusebox. He let me keep the glass fuses, which I turned over in my hands because they were so beautiful. He slammed one on the ground, though, and with his fingers, pinched out a fingernail of copper. We walked through the house. Hangers banged in the closet. Water dripped from the faucet, and flies coupled on the lips of forgotten spoons. A crate of green oranges sat in the washroom. I sat on a stool and looked through *Life* while Uncle climbed into the attic and came down with dust on his eyelashes.

We looked for three hours and returned home. Uncle's shirt was wet under his arms. My shirt of giraffe, elephant, and lion prints was just dusty. When Uncle pulled his shirt over his head, I unbuttoned mine and let the breeze that lived around the almond tree cool my stomach. I looked at Uncle's stomach, which was pinched with muscle. His arms held tattoos of panthers with blood-red claws, and his arm said in blue: "Korea."

The twigs of copper lay on the grass. There wasn't enough copper for a machine to stamp more than a dollar's worth of pennies. Uncle washed his shirt in the garden hose, wrung it hard, and hung it in the tree. An hour later, I got to wear it around the house and twice around the block.

PART TWO

THE INNER TUBE

The tractor inner tube hung in defeat on a nail, accompanied by three flies swinging back and forth, sentries of all that goes unused in a garage. The heat was oppressive for July, especially so for a one-car garage full of the smells of paint remover and open jars of red salmon eggs. I stepped over boxes of old clothes and warped magazines, a lawn mower, and oily engine parts. I kicked over a lamp shade, the bulb bursting its brittle glass, and pushed aside fishing tackle. I reached for the inner tube and touched the rigging of a spider web. I pulled it off quickly and leaped through the debris to the patio. Sweat flooded my face and forked down my arms. I grabbed our hose and washed the inner tube, a slack mouth that I carried over my shoulder to a friend's house.

David had a tire patch kit. He inflated the inner tube with a bicycle pump, and it filled unevenly, one side growing fat like a swollen mouth back-handed by a mean brother. He let the air out, stomped it flat as a shadow, and tried again. Again the air swelled to one side. We stared at the inner tube in confusion.

I asked, "What's wrong with it?"

David didn't say anything. Instead, he jumped up and down on the fat side, but although I joined his weight, laughing as I jumped, the air wouldn't move to the skinny side. After that, we stopped because there was no time to waste. Kathy's pool party was at 1:00, and it was already a quarter after twelve.

We lowered our ears and listened for the hiss of air.

"Put your finger there," David said once we found the puncture. I licked a finger and pressed it into the deflating tube while he squeezed the glue and got the matches ready. But first he scratched the puncture so the patch would stick. I removed my finger, and he buffed the tube back and forth with the rough lid of the tire patch kit. He then smeared the glue and lit the match, the blue flame exciting us for a few seconds. He quickly fit the patch over the puncture and counted to twenty before taking his finger away. We lassoed the inner tube, now nearly deflated, onto the handlebars of my bicycle.

We sat under his cool sycamore waiting for the patch to dry. I asked David what went on at a "pool party," and he said he thought there would be cake and ice cream and races in the pool. I thought about this for a while. The only party that I knew was a birthday party, so when I received an invitation in the mail to a "pool party," I thought it involved the kind of *pool* that my stepfather and uncle shot at Uncle Tom's Tavern. After I caught on, I began to plan what to wear and what to take. I had a snorkel and fins, but my brother had lent the snorkel to his loudmouth friends and it disgusted me that I should fill my mouth with the rubber thing that others had sucked in dirty canals. And the fins were too small; they left painful rings on the insteps of my feet. At the last minute I remembered the inner tube.

David and I got up and poked the patch tenderly, as if it were a wound. The inner tube was healed. He pumped it up until it was huge, and a hollow *thump* resounded when I flicked a finger against the taut skin. I got on my bicycle, and with the inner tube crossed over my shoulder, David gave me a good push. The bike wobbled, but straightened as my legs strained for speed. I was off to a "pool party."

By the time I arrived I was sweaty and nearly dead from not seeing oncoming cars, because every time I turned left the inner tube blocked my view of the road.

The mother who answered the door clapped her hands and said, "Wow!" When I had difficulty getting the inner tube through the front door, she suggested that I go along the side of the house to the backyard. I rolled and pushed and lugged the inner tube, and when everyone saw me come around a bush, they yelled, "Gary's got a tire." I was more than sweaty. My once clean T-shirt was now smeared black along the front, and my hair, earlier parted on the right side and smelling sweetly of Wildroot hair cream, was flat as a blown-over hut. I licked my lips and tasted the hair cream.

When Kathy said hello, I waved my invitation at her and told her I nearly got killed by three cars. Then I jumped into the pool and stayed under for a long time. I was hot, so oiled up by the two-mile ride with an inner tube over my shoulder. I surfaced, got out, and threw the tube in the water. Someone asked, "How come it's big on one side?"

I shrugged, leaped in, and came up among an armada of pink and yellow air mattresses and an inflated plastic swan with a drooping neck. I tried to climb onto the swan, but it sank under my weight. I swam over to my tube, which was like a doctor's couch on the water, huge and plush. Two boys joined me, then a girl, and finally, Kathy and her best friend. We floated around the pool, pushing aside the air mattresses and dunking the plastic swan for good. We stood up on the tube, the boys on the fat side, the girls on the skinny side, and bounced up and down, sometimes falling off but quickly climbing back on. We jumped and laughed, until a toe peeled off the patch and our feet began to mash the deflating tube. Stinky bubbles hissed on the water, and we began to sink, very slowly and happily.

The "pool party" was more than cake and ice cream. We had burgers as well, with potato chips and plenty of punch. I swam as much as I could. By the time I left—the last boy to go home—my eyes were red and my hair was parted down the middle from diving a hundred times into the pool. I enjoyed a cool ride home with the breathless inner tube hanging exhausted around my neck.

THE PIE

I knew enough about hell to stop me from stealing. I was holy in almost every bone. Some days I recognized the shadows of angels flopping on the backyard grass, and other days I heard faraway messages in the plumbing that howled underneath the house when I crawled there looking for something to do.

But boredom made me sin. Once, at the German Market, I stood before a rack of pies, my sweet tooth gleaming and the juice of guilt wetting my underarms. I gazed at the nine kinds of pie, pecan and apple being my favorites, although cherry looked good, and my dear, fat-faced chocolate was always a good bet. I nearly wept trying to decide which to steal and, forgetting the flowery dust priests give off, the shadow of angels and the proximity of God howling in the plumbing underneath the house, sneaked a pie behind my coffee-lid Frisbee and walked to the door, grinning to the bald grocer whose forehead shone with a window of light.

"No one saw," I muttered to myself, the pie like a discus in my hand, and hurried across the street, where I sat on someone's lawn. The sun wavered between the branches of a yellowish sycamore. A squirrel nailed itself high on the trunk, where it forked into two large bark-scabbed limbs. Just as I was going to work my cleanest finger into the pie, a neighbor came out to the porch for his mail. He looked at me, and I got up and headed for home. I raced on skinny legs to my block, but slowed to a quick walk when I couldn't wait any longer. I held the pie to my nose and breathed in its sweetness. I licked some of the crust and closed my eyes as I took a small bite.

In my front yard, I leaned against a car fender and panicked about stealing the apple pie. I knew an apple got Eve in deep trouble with snakes because Sister Marie had shown us a film about Adam and Eve being cast into the desert, and what scared me more than falling from grace was being thirsty for the rest of my life. But even that didn't stop me from clawing a chunk from the pie tin and pushing it into the cavern of my mouth. The slop was sweet and gold-colored in the afternoon sun. I laid more pieces on my tongue, wet finger-dripping pieces, until I was finished and felt like crying because it was about the best thing I had ever tasted. I realized right there and then, in my sixth year, in my tiny body of two hundred bones and three or four sins, that the best things in life came stolen. I wiped my sticky fingers on the grass and rolled my tongue over the corners of my mouth. A burp perfumed the air.

I felt bad not sharing with Cross-Eyed Johnny, a neighbor kid. He stood over my shoulder and asked, "Can I have some?" Crust fell from my mouth, and my teeth were bathed with the jam-like filling. Tears blurred my eyes as I remembered the grocer's forehead. I remembered the other pies on the rack, the warm air of the fan above the door and the car that honked as I crossed the street without looking.

"Get away," I had answered Cross-Eyed Johnny. He watched my fingers greedily push big chunks of pie down my throat. He swallowed and said in a whisper, "Your hands are dirty," then returned home to climb his roof and sit watching me eat the pie by myself. After a while, he jumped off and hobbled away because the fall had hurt him.

I sat on the curb. The pie tin glared at me and rolled away when the wind picked up. My face was sticky with guilt. A car honked, and the driver knew. Mrs. Hancock stood on her lawn, hands on hip, and she knew. My mom, peeling a mountain of potatoes at the Redi-Spud factory, knew. I got to my feet, stomach taut, mouth tired of chewing, and flung my Frisbee across the street, its shadow like the shadow of an angel fleeing bad deeds. I retrieved it, jogging slowly. I flung it again until I was bored and thirsty.

I returned home to drink water and help my sister glue bottle caps onto cardboard, a project for summer school. But the bottle caps bored me, and the water soon filled me up more than the pie. With the kitchen stifling with heat and lunatic flies, I decided to crawl underneath our house and lie in the cool shadows listening to the howling sound of plumbing. Was it God? Was it Father, speaking from death, or Uncle with his last shiny dime? I listened, ear pressed to a cold pipe, and heard a howl like the sea. I lay until I was cold and then crawled back to the light, rising from one knee, then another, to dust off my pants and squint in the harsh light. I looked and saw the glare of a pie tin on a hot day. I knew sin was what you took and didn't give back.

THE HAIRCUT

Rhinehardt, twelve-year-old barber, dropped my mother's sewing scissors on the floor and ran out of the house, leaving me in the kitchen blinking the small eyes of a dull chicken. My hair lay in the dish towel wrapped around my shoulders and on the floor, with a few renegade strands floating through the air. I got up and looked in the hall mirror. My new haircut had all kinds of weird angles. It parted on the right, the left, and even down the center. My scalp was bluish, and with so much hair gone, my nose was huge as an evil root. I'm going to get that Okie, I promised myself. I swept the floor and snapped the towel on the back porch. I chased down some floating hair strands and went outside to look for him.

The sun glared on the asphalt. The street was empty of kids and dogs. Mrs. Prince was whacking a dust mop on a holly bush. I walked down to Romain playground, which, except around the pool, looked deserted. I borrowed Caveman's swimming trunks. He was through swimming for the day, so I decided to postpone my hunt for Rhinehardt and jumped into the public pool full of fifty Mexican kids beating the blue water white. My school friend, Alfonso, swam crocodile style, his mouth and nose underwater and his eyes on the surface. He stood up and asked about my head. I explained it was a new haircut, and he ran a finger through one of the parts. I pushed him away, and he returned to his crocodile swim.

I stayed most of that afternoon on the bottom of the pool, avoiding my brother and sister, who had shown up with towels over their shoulders. I liked the sound of kicking legs and the dream-like sight of other kids holding their breath underwater with eyes open and seaweed hair wavering about. I came up for air, looked around at the racket, and sank once more to the bottom of the deep end of the pool where the water was cleaner from not being touched.

Exhausted and red-eyed from the chlorine, I got out after two hours, changed in the gray shadows of the men's room, and returned the swimming trunks to Caveman, who was playing Ping-Pong with a crushed ball. My brother, Rick, already dry from swimming, looked at my haircut and asked, "What happened?" I ignored him and played Sorry, then four square. Finally, a knot of hunger in my stomach, I returned home racing from patch to patch of shade. Like a dummy, I had forgotten my shoes.

I had also forgotten about my haircut. Mom was at the stove with steamed-up eyeglasses, refrying beans with one hand on her hip. Over dinner the fog cleared from her lenses and she asked, "What happened to your hair?"

I touched the top of my head, shocked, mouth open to reveal bits of half-chomped tortilla. I remembered Rhinehardt chuckling and hair parachuting to the floor. I remembered the cold scissors around my ears. Mom puckered her mouth into a bud of angry lines. She ripped her tortilla and said she would fix me later.

After dinner, she cut the rest of my hair on the backyard lawn, yanked roughly at each snip, and left me as bald as the belly of a boneless chicken.

I looked in the mirror and scared myself. Hate was in my heart, and I imagined Rhinehardt sitting in his own kitchen with a towel around his neck. I felt better only after Mother said we were having Kool-Aid ice cubes for dessert. I sucked on three cherry-flavored cubes in the backyard and did cartwheels with my sister.

I tried to forget about my hair. My palms tingled when I raked them over the bristles. My brother didn't tease me because he was feeling too sad about his girlfriend moving away. My stepfather, home late from work and red in the face from drinking at Uncle Tom's Tavern, grinned at me as he held onto the wall. He said he liked my hair because it made me look like a Marine. He dug into his pocket for some change and handed me a nickel, three pennies, and his nail clippers. His eyes floated in alcohol. He looked at the nail clippers and then said, "I got one like that."

Before I got into bed, I curled thirty-pound weights in the garage under the halo of a twenty-watt bulb, feeling strong because a ribbon of sweat began to run from my armpits. I was sure that if my mother were trapped under a car wheel, I could save her with my leg strength. I stood in front of the mirror. My head didn't look that bad. I was as lean as Mrs. Prince's dust mop, but strong, I thought. I made a shiny muscle in my right arm and bared my teeth all the way to my gums. I ran a hand through my baldness. For three weeks, smooth was my favorite feeling.

THE CONFESSION

The first time I confessed, I admitted throwing bubble gum into a bush. The priest, Monsignor Singleton, asked, What else? I told him I called my sister terrible names and broke a just-opened jar of pickles, for which I received a spanking that caused hate in my heart for a good two hours. Monsignor smacked his lips and asked, "OK, what else?" I stuttered when I told him that I had stolen sunflower seeds from Ann's Liquors and lied to my teacher when I told her that I had once entered a cave and found fool's gold clinging to the ceiling.

Monsignor's rosary banged against the wall as he shifted on his sore knees. He breathed deeply and asked, "Is there more?" I confessed pounding a Coke machine until it burped a quarter, and confessed having thoughts about stealing more bags of sunflower seeds because it would make me popular with the older boys on my block.

The priest nodded his head, and when he spoke, gave off the scent of a dry flower. I tried not looking at him through the wispy screen of right and wrong. I looked down at my hands. The air was dry as a twig, and dark but not so dark that I couldn't make out ballpoint scribbling on the little shelf where my hands rested in prayer. I was shocked, and began to think of my own ballpoint pen, which I loved for its chrome band which I sometimes wore on my pinky and sometimes sucked until it left a ring on my tongue. I also loved the spring that jumped up and down, and the reservoir of receding ink. I must have learned a lot that year because most of the ink was gone.

And now this scribbling. My pen jabbed the inside of my pocket. I knew I was in trouble because I always remembered too late and was spanked from one room to the next. I began to think that maybe I had done the scribbling while waiting in the dark for my turn to say confession. That had been the story of my third-grade life. If I poured from a half-gallon of milk in the morning, when I returned home from the playground, scuffed by grass and soccer balls, I would find the milk sitting in a triangle of sunlight. If I turned on the sprinkler, I would come home hours later to find the gutters running warm, murky water and my mother standing, hands on hips, behind the front window. I sometimes left my baby brother in his high chair for three hours before I remembered him. I would go to school without lunch, then remember. I would forget a book on the bus and cry because anytime Mother had to open her purse to pay for something I lost, I knew I was in big trouble.

The priest spoke kindly. He said I was a good boy but could be better if I would go back to the bush and pick up that piece of bubble gum. I said, "Yes, Father," and got tongue-tied when I started the Act of Contrition. Father helped me along, word by word, and then, sighing the scent of dry flowers, slid the sliding door shut. In the dark, I wet my fingers with spit and rubbed out the scribbling as best as I could.

I sneezed when I left the confessional. The air was cool with the draft of shadows where saints lurked with armfuls of snakes and half-bitten apples. The next boy was mumbling, his sins I suspected, and his shirt buttons were in the wrong holes. Kenneth Colombini, the class idiot who spent most of his school life in the wastepaper basket, asked, "How did it taste?"

"What do you mean?"

"The Host." I made a face and said, "You better not scribble in there."

Kenneth's arm was blue with ink markings. A line, like blood poisoning, ran up his forearm, and his name, "Ken the Great," circled his wrist. Some blue was smeared around his mouth from sucking his pen. He slowly raised his palm to reveal the face of a laughing clown. He laughed until his chest heaved with a bronchial disease and then disappeared into the confessional, nearly slamming the door.

I said three Hail Marys and one Our Father, looked around at the paintings of tortured saints, and closed my eyes when I heard a rap in the confessional and Monsignor scolding Kenneth. Poor, dumb Kenneth. He was on his knees now, confessing to popping two erasers in Sister Marie's face.

I left with a drip of holy water on my forehead. Outside, the sky was bluish-gray and the wind was ripping petals from rose bushes. I looked at my hands and a prick of guilt made me jump. They were blue from a ballpoint pen. I thought of Kenneth Colombini, the laughing clown on his palm, and winced at the thought that I might be like him.

On the way home I had to look behind three bushes, each one more wicked with thorns than the next, before I found a wad of gum. It was gray, not pink like bubble gum, but I knew it was better to clean up another kid's sin than to let it lie forever in the earth, the house of the eyeless worm.

THE CATFISH

Roeding Park was five miles from home, far enough for me to act goofy and spit the shells of sunflower seeds during a hard-pedaling bike ride. A shell stuck to my forehead, and another clung like a fly to my cheek before the wind ripped it off. I let the one on my forehead stay until I got off my bike, sweaty and tired, and walked to a pond where black kids in collarless T-shirts fished.

I stopped to watch them awhile, cautiously holding onto my bike because I was afraid one of them might throw down his pole and pedal off with what was mine. The kidney-shaped pond rippled with mosquitoes and water skeeters, and paper cups and ice cream wrappers floated near the edges. I left and climbed a gold-painted Sherman tank, also littered with paper cups and wrappers, the turret slashed with initials and dumb faces. The sun, yellow as a tooth, was already above the trees, the shadows leaning west instead of east as they do when the sun goes down. Although it was a weekday, some families were banging aluminum folding chairs from station wagons. One man was carrying an ice chest on his shoulder. A couple was smoothing an army blanket, placing a heavy object at each corner—purse, ice chest, two soft tennis shoes—so the wind would not peel it back.

From the tank I rode to the zoo. I didn't have

fifty cents to get in, so I leaned my bike against the
chain link fence and listened to the hyena laugh.
The king of the jungle was sleeping, no doubt, and
his kin, the spotted and black panthers, were pac-
ing their stinky cages like mad doctors. The rhino
was bathing in lukewarm mud, and the elephant
and the giant turtle were doing nothing. The black
bear was doing next to nothing, except yawning
on a cement rock, and bantam roosters were pecking at the sandy ground where the gazelles ran
with their young.

But I could imagine for only so long. I brought
my palms to my face and inhaled deeply the salt of
sunflower seeds and the long, sweaty ride. I was
hungry. I had eaten cereal before I left home but
now it was a little after eleven, and I was hungry. I
pinched the last few sunflower seeds from my
pockets and chewed them, shell and all, as I returned to the pond where there was now only one
kid fishing. I dropped my bike on the lawn. I
looked in his pail and saw three catfish looking up
at me, their Fu Manchu whiskers brushed back,
and an occasional burst of bubbles rising from
their turned down mouths.

Without thinking, I asked the boy if he had ever
eaten a sugar cane. He looked up, one eye squinting from the sun, and said, "What's that?"

After I took great lengths to describe the cane,
the sweetness and woody fiber you could swallow
without getting sick, he said "No." I told him it
cost twenty-five cents a foot, and measured a foot
with my hands. He returned his gaze to the water
without answering. I got down on one knee and

looked, too. I was going to say a few more things about sugar cane when the line jerked and a catfish the color of a black shoe suddenly rose from the brackish water.

I jumped to my feet, scared. The kid took a few steps away from the pond, the pole moving like a crane and hovering over the lawn. Then the catfish was lowered and allowed to flop and smother itself in flakes of grass. Its gills opened and closed, a wound healing itself, and his bluish fangs munched on the fish hook.

We watched the catfish, mesmerized. I asked if I could undo the hook, and he asked where he could get sugar cane. I pointed to the Christian school across from Roeding Park. "A girl from where I live goes there, and she sold me some." He looked at the school but said nothing.

I got down on my knees, careful not to scrape my hand against the whiskers because I had heard my stepfather say they were like razor blades. The catfish's eyes were fogged, scratched I assumed from turning over and over on the lawn. It was gasping, and when I looked into its gaping mouth I saw that its insides were mostly dark air. When I gripped the catfish and found it was icy cold, I stood back up quickly.

The kid unhooked the catfish. I picked up my bike and left, not nearly as happy as when I started off. That night, I opened my stepfather's tackle box and studied the furry lures and spinners. I took a plain hook and worked the point under my thumb, peeling away a little skin as if I had a sliver and was probing with a sewing needle. I didn't have to draw blood to know it would hurt.

I went to bed thinking that only so much meat hangs on a spine. When I closed my eyes, the cat-fish stared at me, then flopped over and stared at me again.

THE IN-BETWEEN DINNER SNACKS

It only took one BB from an air gun to bring down a pigeon, and ten fingers to pull the feathers from its bony frame. Arnold, my mentor of poor days, showed me how. He stood in the cool shadows of his backyard, brushed his hair back with a hand, aimed, and a pigeon on a wire dropped like ripe fruit. It looked around, hurt, its wings fluttering like a piece of a gray sea, its eyes like the eyes of something far away. Arnold's thumb and index finger stopped that bird from breathing. I ran away because I didn't like the way things were going.

My barefoot brother was across the street at Coleman Pickle fishing large pickles from the open barrels. He climbed into a barrel, the green water sloshing the rim, and said that it felt weird stepping on pickles. It's like floating, he said, and squeezed his toes around a pickle and brought it to the surface. The pickle was large as a trout, green as something sick. I backed away when he threw it at me.

I ran home where I found Sister on the just-painted back porch. She was trying to crack an almond with her teeth. Her face was bunched up, one eye squinted into a pirate's wink. The almond creaked under the back-row anger of baby teeth. When I told her she was sitting on wet paint, she started crying. The almond glistened in her mouth, and for a moment I thought she was going to swallow it and choke. I told her to spit it out and she shook her ponytails, saying, "It's mine."

The life of a five-year-old lay between Coleman Pickle and the Molinas' house. But when Mom wasn't looking, my brother and I sometimes risked going down to the 7-Up Bottling Company and standing in the entrance of the warehouse until one of the workers brought us an icy drink. Knowing that Sister was in big trouble, that Mother would scold her and then wash her, that I had at least a half-hour for monkey business, I crossed the street and fetched my brother who was now walking tightrope on the skylight of Coleman Pickle.

"Deb's in trouble," I yelled in the funnel of cupped hands. "She sat on paint."

He climbed down and we raced over to 7-Up Bottling. My brother stunk of pickles, but I was pretty clean. We waited at attention, and finally, a worker in a blue shirt said, "What kind today?"

I got a 7-Up and my brother a Frosty root beer because he liked the way the froth lathered his

upper lip. He agreed that 7-Up burned the nostrils
and made more burps, but root beer was an older
boy's drink. We drank eyeing each other and tell-
ing the other his drink was better. Finished, we
placed the bottles in a wooden rack and raced
back home. Mother was washing Deb with the
garden hose in the backyard. We looked at her and
said, "We didn't go anywhere."

She sprayed us with the hose, and said, *"Men-
tirosos!"* Because it was summer, because a necklace of dirt darkened our chicken-skinny necks,
we didn't move until the water was flushing out
our eyes and we couldn't breathe anymore.

I returned to the Molinas' house. Arnold was
inside stirring soup with a yellow pencil. I stood on
tip-toe and looked in. The pigeon's head was bobbing as it carouseled in the current of brownish
water. Three chopped carrots bobbed as well, and
an armada of diced celery. He gave three shakes of
salt, one of pepper, one of something else, and
added a leaf from a jar. The pigeon bobbed in the
whirlpool, and I watched it until I got dizzy.

I left Arnold and joined kids rolling a bowling
ball in the hallway. The game was to jump at the
last minute as it approached the pins—us kids
standing at attention. The ball started off slowly,
ricochetting off the walls, but by the time it
reached us it was going fast. I played until the
bowling ball knocked over one of the bigger babies, and I knew it was smart to get the hell out. I
was already outside when the baby caught her
breath and had enough air to start crying.

I returned home and sat on the porch but

jumped up when I realized it was wet. My bottom was sticky, but not really paint-stained. The afternoon sun had dried it in a matter of hours. When a car honked, I went out to the front of the house. It was Mrs. Garcia, a friend of the family, in her banged-up station wagon. She was laughing before anyone said anything, happy I guess because she had just finished her shift at the noodle factory. She was there to take care of us because Mother was going out for the evening.

Mother descended the porch with cigarette smoke squinting her eyes. She patted Mrs. Garcia's freckled arm that was propped outside the window. She told us kids to get in the car. We knew Mrs. Garcia. We knew her broken down house and the dirt that scudded across the floor when the front door opened and closed. Rick made a face, but followed Debra and me. In the back seat, the three of us made even uglier faces. Two of Mrs. Garcia's babies were jumping up and down in five-gallon tubs of chow mein. I looked at the noodles squirm like snakes and make the sound of snails being pulled apart. I felt sick because I knew Mrs. Garcia was going to try to feed noodles to us for dinner, but I was so glad that I had eaten earlier in the day.

The three of us made sour faces at the babies. Rick didn't smell so much of pickles because he had changed his shirt and pants, and Mother had washed him clean with a garden hose. He was dressed for dinner, and even his hair lay flat. Mrs. Garcia laughed when one of the babies climbed from the back to help put the car in reverse. Mrs.

Garcia worked the brake and gas pedal and the
baby did most of the steering. We moved down the
street in fits, and while we were miserable the
Garcias were happy to get going. They were looking forward to a square meal from the round tubs
in the back seat.

THE CHICKS

At first the three chicks were little puffs of yellow dandelion floating in our backyard, squeaking
like rusty latches. I followed after them in big flapping tennis shoes and eleven-year-old awkward-
ness, happy because they were newborn and
breathing the April air of blossoms and hope. They
didn't seem to do much. They pecked at the sandy
ground and flapped their tiny wings. They blinked
a lot, too, scratched, and went to sleep standing
up. When one started moving, the others followed. They traveled in threes with quick neck-
bobbing jerks. I thought it cute that they liked to
climb onto my feet until one shit on my tennis
shoe and I had to clean it off on the grass. I kicked
sand in the chick's face but immediately felt sorry
for him because he didn't stop blinking for the
longest time.

By the third week they were large and grayish-
yellow with the start of red combs on the tops of
their heads. I no longer fed them grain from my

outspread palm or held up leaves of lettuce for them to perforate with their beaks. The mayonnaise lid I used for their water trough was replaced by a plastic dish. I no longer raced after them. Rick, my older brother, said it was stupid to care for them.

But I had to. They had outgrown their cardboard pen, and I couldn't just leave them because the neighbor's cat had sniffed them out. With wire and some mismatched lumber, I made a new pen. And just in time. The cat had attacked a chick, which gave up a few feathers and screams but no blood. Or so I thought. The next day when I let them out to "play," the hurt chick seemed dizzy and quiet. His blink was slow. One wing seemed bent. I patted its nub of comb and purred, "What's wrong?"

I went inside the house to do the dishes and when I returned, the neighbor's cat was carrying the hurt chick over the fence. I threw a rock at the cat, and cuss words. I hated myself for leaving the chick alone. I sat down on the ground while the two other chickens continued dropping their round chicken turds in the dust. I stirred the ground with a stick and felt a great hatred for the cat. I didn't even have its body to bury, or a name to call it.

When they were a month old, the chicks, now named Henrietta and Willy, began to walk like chickens, high-stepping in the weeds and tomato plants. They began to sound like chickens too, clucking instead of squeaking. They also shit more. They became nasty, and when my younger brother tried to play with them, Henrietta pecked his belly button, which was showing under his T-shirt. Blood sprang skyward, and my brother, mouth open in shock, began to cry. Fortunately, my mother wasn't home. I washed his belly button and fit a flesh-colored, circle Band-Aid on his wound. I was scared because I thought that maybe his belly button would rip open and his guts would flood out. Then I would really be in trouble.

The chicks were now dusty white chickens. Although they were huge and scary, the neighbor's cat still hungered for them. I was still pained by the death of the first one. I decided to get my revenge by hiding behind a fort of cardboard while the two remaining chickens scratched about the yard. I waited with sweaty rocks in my hand. Finally, the cat climbed onto the fence, jumped down, and creeped toward Willy, who just looked and blinked at the cat. I rose quickly and threw a rock but missed. I threw others and missed, cussed, and climbed the fence to shout at the cat, which disappeared behind car parts.

I shepherded the two remaining chickens that had grown huge and so wildly stupid that they began to shit in their drinking water and peck the hand that fed them. I hit them with a mop, chased them, and was angry because they were so unappreciative of my concern for them. I would stay with them for hours, sweating under the early summer sun. I would spend my own pennies for a pinch of grain. I would walk to Country Boy Market where, shamefaced, I asked the grocer for wilted lettuce.

Because I was careless, Willy was the next to get it. Instead of carrying him away, the cat ripped into the chicken in our vegetable garden. His whiskers were bloody, his eyes narrow, his jaw white with feathers. I threw the mop at the cat and missed. I climbed the fence and went looking for the cat, calling "Here, kittykittykitty." I returned to scoop Willy onto a shovel and bury him in the corner of the yard. Tears flooded my eyes. While I whittled a cross, Henrietta went about pecking grain and lettuce, unmoved by the passing of her friend Willy.

But Henrietta had her day. I became less and less interested in the preservation of my last chick, that onetime little puff of feathers. I was playing dodgeball in the front yard when I heard a chicken cry and raced to find the cat dragging the fluttering Henrietta across the yard. When the cat saw me, he let go and climbed the fence in two leaps.

Henrietta was badly hurt. I tried to catch and comfort her, but she trotted around the yard, trailing loose feathers and blood. Toward evening, she finally quieted and allowed me to pick her up, coo at her earless head, and place her in the pen. The next morning, she was very quiet when I let her out. She walked with a limp, but mostly sat blinking. She didn't eat or drink from her dish. Her beak seemed more open than closed, and for the first time I saw that a chicken's tongue was stiff, like a matchstick.

The following days she dragged herself about on her good leg, and a day later she couldn't flutter her wings. My brother said we had to chop off her head. I was scared, and my brother was scared. I picked up Henrietta and said, "I'm sorry," and cuddled her as I carried her to a two-by-four set on bricks. I let her go at the last minute and told Rick that I couldn't do it. He couldn't do it either, and we sat on the grass, feeling awful as we listened to the chicken beat about on the ground. When I turned around, Henrietta was blinking her eyes at us.

Rick hit me hard in the arm and said it was my fault. He rose quickly, grabbed the shovel, and with three sloppy strikes and a lot of anger, Henrietta's neck came off and warm blood and feathers mingled with the grassy weeds. Rick threw down the shovel. I started crying because it was now my job to bury her. I scooped up her body on the shovel, then her closed-eyed head, and buried her next to Willy.

I didn't fit a cross over her grave until the following day. I pushed over the pen, flattening it by jumping up and down on it. For the rest of the summer the neighbor's cat climbed onto the fence every day to see if we had more chickens.

THE NEW AND
OLD TENNIES

Mother looks up from stirring dinner in a black pan, her hips cha-chaing under a chicken-print apron. A smell has touched her. She knows it from somewhere, but where? She taps her spoon against the pan and looks at her son with watered-down hair. He's a sloppy boy with sloppy posture which neither the nuns nor a strict father could correct. Moons of dirt dwell under his fingernails. His teeth are pasty. His arms are blue with the tattoos of pen markings.

Earlier in the day he had walked in a wet field and stepped on something soft. He scraped the bottoms of his new tennis shoes as best he could and continued an incline of mushroom-dark hills, the ropes of his leg muscles tightening, his breath shallow. The canal was west behind the trees, where the leaves mulched in the shadows. Leprous frogs lived in leaf-spotted water, and the fish, dulled by chemicals, floated near the oily surface, their tails waving weakly, their gills like raw, pink-ish wounds. He could have walked waist-deep into the canal, cupped a fish in his palm, and shared its misery. But the boy knew better. His mother would have scolded him for getting wet. So he walked along the canal bank, dull as the fish, and

threw rocks and watched the rippling targets di-
late. He hunched on the bank and wished winter
would rise from the mountains, white as a nurse's
hat. Then he could wear two socks on each foot
and crunch the miles of frost with his shoes. Then
he could slide on the ice and risk his face playing
front-yard football.

Nothing sticks to the smooth bottoms of red tennis shoes like the scent of squashed bugs and this-
tle. The shoes are quiet, slick from the wear of
climbing trees, and scuffed at the toe from kicking
the boredom out of curbs. They are quick, though,
swift enough to outdistance the orange-haired sister of the school bully. She would like to kiss him,
drink from his neck, hug him and feel the air that
lives in the deepest cells of his lungs.

Worn tennies. They smell of summer grass,
asphalt, a moist sock breathing the defeat of baseball. He was no good in third grade, and now, in
the sixth, he's still awful at the game. He blames
the bat, the sloshed ball, and the sun angling
sparks off the fence. He blames the pitcher, a fat
kid who hides the ball in the wide screen of his
gray T-shirt. His mother was wrong in marrying
his thin-armed father who bared his teeth and
grunted when he opened fresh bottles of ketchup.
And his older brother was piggish for getting all
the warm milk, all the best cuts of meat. Most of
the players, the Lions, didn't get any milk or meat
either. They are weak at bat and can't tell the
difference between a ball and a piece of paper
blowing across the field.

The shoes are grass-stained and itchy with

foxtails and burrs. Sand had crept into the toe, and no matter how he pounds the tennis shoes against the curb, he can still feel the fine grains against his socks. The laces are gray and slack, and the rubber label that says P. F. Flyers is missing. It came off when the orange-haired sister caught up to him and filled his neck with kisses. She ripped off the label, said, "You're mine forever," and left him sucking air because she was stronger than he had ever imagined. She had squeezed all his air and tasted his candy-red tongue.

He floated the shoes in a metal pail, two red fish that stunk of forty days and forty nights. He drowned them in detergent and hung them on a clothesline, dirty tears dripping from the laces. Meanwhile, he wore dress-up shoes and paced the floor, waiting for the sun to starch the tennies dry and stiff as a twig so he could wear them loose racing the base paths in a runaway game.

With worn tennies, the kid could sneak into ten o'clock mass when he's late. He could leap rose bushes and puddles. He could leap onto a boat as it pulled away and be the first to leap onto the dock when it returned, the deep-throated motor gurgling black water. With worn tennies, he has been somewhere. He has climbed and run, and run to climb onto graffiti-sprayed rocks. He has played good basketball on a lousy team, shopped with his mother, who can't believe her luck that no shoe fits, and has been stopped by dogs who will sniff and remember him for what he is—a rough hand on the collar, a kind slap on a dusty coat, a call to a bone with its strings of beautifully fleshed meat.

At night, moonlight spears the bedroom floor, the chest of drawers, and a pile of jeans and T-shirts. The tennies lay like struck animals on the side of the road. But they are warm and soft as they let off the steam of a full day.

THE GUARDIAN ANGEL

A guardian angel may follow you along a rust-colored river, up telephone poles to those humming canisters, or through hedges and vines where thirsty dogs pant. He may hover over a line of wet laundry, cleaning a fingernail and whistling for his own enchantment. He may even be that blue vapor issuing from a tailpipe of a car idling in the road. Guardian angels are always near, or so I was told by my mother, who also believed in fortunes laid out on a gypsy's wobbly card table.

But when my brother got his pants leg caught on the top of a high fence and hung upside down, weeping and muttering curses because his pants were newly torn and Mother would spank him for sure, no angel was with him. His guardian angel was asleep or dull-witted. He also snoozed when a pine cone hit my brother in the face, right under the left eye, which, along with the right eye, was looking skyward at a milk-throated bird he intended to bring down with a rock. My brother's guardian slept when he and a friend played Frisbee with a tin coffee lid, and when a pan of boiling water splashed on his leg. But he did wake up in time to pull the steering wheel as he fell asleep. Three buddies were in the back, all boozed and stinking of the failure of the Giants to hit with men on.

It was tough luck for my brother. He chipped a tooth, broke one arm, then the other, and stepped on every tack in the house. Blood poisoning ran like a mouse up his arm, and knife-wielding *cholos* chased him from junior high to high school. And things kept falling on him from the sky: limbs from a diseased tree, rocks hurled from the neighbor's yard, and a virus that had him in bed for months, his eyes like the eyes of a sad panda.

My guardian angel was a light sleeper. He saved me from speeding cars, playground fights, and mercury splashing in my face. That was in fifth grade when we stole balls of mercury from the science teacher to shine coins and belt buckles. Finished, we closed one eye and flung the mercury at each another and giggled all the way to lunch.

He saved me from Frankie T., the schoolyard terrorist, and the pain of having my Valentine lollipop crunched loudly in my ear by the wrong girl. He saved me from taking a baseball in the face. He breathed "No" in my ear when I was popping open my mother's coin purse where bitter pennies slept.

Three times I was supposed to die. The last time, I fell off a waterfall, God knows how many feet. The ride over rock and slimy moss scared me. Just

as on TV, I saw my life flash before me. For me, life
was mostly summer days tramping in cut-offs and
a peach-stained T-shirt. I loved my life, and loved
playing and eating the same meal over and over
and even the loneliness of a thirteen-year-old in
jeans bursting with love. I survived, though. I
sprained an ankle, limped for two weeks until the
sparks of pain stopped, and then decided I should
limp the rest of the summer because girls seemed
to notice hurt guys.

Now I need my guardian angel more than ever.
My soul is filled with holes, and both knees hurt
from years of karate. Sometimes I scare my black
brothers, but mostly they chase me around the
karate floor because I'm the black belt with low
kicks and wimpy punches. They hit and kick me,
but not too hard because they know I'm the only
one with a good job. They're struggling to live on a
jingle of quarters, dimes, and green pennies. They
just want to scare me, to send me driving home
with a footprint on my chest. I enjoy showering
and then sitting in the living room, nursing my
welts with a cold beer in my hand.

Motorcycles scare me. From the front window, I
see them speed by, reckless as stars let go from
heaven. Sports cars scare me too, and dogs with
mismatched eyes, widows in black, and fungus on
newly picked apples. I'm suspicious of candles that
sputter in church. Sometimes when I look up from
prayer at 5:30 mass, I see a candle waver and go
dead, sending up a spine of smoke. God is looking,
I feel, the Lord is letting go of another meager
soul. I clear my throat and think that someone is

not being prayed for, someone in limbo is receding farther away, a dead father on a rack of dank earth, a mother with the slack smile of a failed life.

My angel was with me for years. I could do as I pleased and return unharmed. Now I'm uncertain. In the backyard, the leaves of the apple tree rattle across the lawn. The pond is black, and the slats of the fence are vented with disease. My friends are far away. Their crisp letters bring a fear of getting old. I close my eyes and pray that I'll know what to do with my free time. I'll listen to my breathing, make it stop and go, and catch the angel off guard. Is he really there? Is he that sigh in the trees? Is he hovering over the clothesline or standing upright among the shovels and hoes? I want nothing more than to be happy by next fall, by the time the orange trees hang heavy with the water of perpetual fruit.

THE FIGHTS

Whenever any aunt or uncle brought out a Brownie camera, my brother and I began fighting. We grunted and wrestled, the hot snot of anger shining our upper lips. We growled, teeth bared, and karate chopped with one eye on the camera. When we fell, our bony elbows ripped holes into their lawns, and worms squirmed to get out of the way. We breathed hard and cussed when a button

came loose. We smiled at our relatives fumbling
for coins in their pockets. We thought people liked
to watch fights, and even better, liked snapshots of
front-yard fights.

I visited my Aunt Jesse on a Saturday and sat on
her long flowery couch, which was sealed in a clear
plastic, and looked through her album of ancient
snapshots also sealed in plastic. I drank from a
ceramic coffee cup, laughed, and spilled four ugly
drops of chocolate on the couch. I moved over,
and let my jeans absorb the drops.

My aunt, chicken-print dish towel in hand,
pulled a chair up next to me, careful not to rake
the legs across her shag carpet. She wiped the
couch and sat down. We pressed our heads together and looked at the photo album. In one
black and white snapshot, I'm on the ground,
balled up like a potato bug. In another, Rick's face
is slurred from a right cross, and in the next Rick
has me in a headlock but both of us are smiling into
the camera. In still another, only my legs are showing, and the shadow of my sister with a pinwheel.
The pinwheel, I remember, was later ripped from
her hand when she hung it outside the car window. I liked the snapshot of Brother and me bar-
ing our new, grown-up teeth to the tops of the
gums. Our fists are held high and Rick's cowlick is
standing up like a feather. And there was one in
which Rick has me pinned to the ground while
blood wiggled from his nose to his cheek. I remember that well. He was mad because an elbow
caught him in the face, and he had to go to our
cousin's wedding with a bloody shirt.

"You kids were really something," my aunt said. She picked up my cup from the end table and wiped the ring of water. When she offered me a cookie, I smiled but refused because a grain or two of crumbled cookie might fall on her rug.

In the same photo album there were nice snapshots of beaches and new cars and houses. Grandfather is standing in front of his avocado tree. Grandmother is pinching aphids from a rose bush. Mexico is a still-water fountain splashing forever in the dusty light of Mexico. My aunt pointed to a distant uncle with a *guitarron* in his arm, and tapped a long red fingernail on the face of the Raisin queen of a 1940s parade. "This is a friend of mine," she said, and then said, "she didn't last long like that," meaning her flat tummy and pointed breasts, meaning her hair piled up and the flashy beauty of straight teeth. She followed my aunt to the cannery and a dull marriage of stewing diapers on the stove.

When I turned the page, we returned once again to brotherly snapshots, this time in color. Rick and I are leaping high from a playground swing, our arms crossed and our faces stern as mad genies. In a creased snapshot, we are flinging down a handful of popcorn to a gray sea of pigeons. Sister's shadow is flat on the ground, minus her pinwheel, and there's the start of another shadow which may well be our mother's.

I bit into one of my aunt's cookies. Three crumbs fell on the rug and immediately she dropped to one arthritic knee. I turned the page of the album. There were photographs of my cousin's wedding in San Jose. No one looks happy or young, except Rick and me. We had discovered the laundry chute and two wet mops that we used as lances as we ran down the hall. We had discovered that we could eat and drink as much as we pleased.

My brother and I loved fighting at family get-togethers. We were lucky not to lose teeth. We didn't bruise easily or break arms when we fell. Neither of us liked the sparks of pain, but neither of us could quite stop windmilling our tiny arms at each other. It was too much fun.

Now at Christmas, we stand next to each other talking about money made and money lost. We open expensive presents and make funny faces into the Polaroid camera when we've drunk too much. Rick likes to bare his teeth, and I like to lower my head slightly so that my eyes roll up like a doll's peering through its frontal lobe. My sister's shadow falls on the wall. I look and catch her licking sweets from one long, red fingernail. She likes to eat, and likes to bring in money. I wonder if she remembers her pinwheel and the time when she stomped a black shoe in a little dance. Back when our uncles stood around fumbling for coins in their pockets. When the days were black and white, and Brownie cameras sucked in a part of our lives through round, smudged lenses.

THE GYMNAST

For three days of my eleventh summer I listened to my mother yap about my cousin, Issac, who was taking gymnastics. She was proud of him, she said one evening at the stove as she pounded a round steak into *carne asada* and crushed a heap of beans into *refritos*. I was jealous because I had watched my share of *Wide World of Sports* and knew that people admired an athlete who could somersault without hurting himself. I pushed aside my solitary game of Chinese checkers and spent a few minutes rolling around the backyard until I was dizzy and itchy with grass.

That Saturday, I went to Issac's house where I ate plums and sat under an aluminum arbor watching my cousin, dressed in gymnastic shorts and top, do spindly cartwheels and backflips in his backyard while he instructed, "This is the correct way." He breathed in the grassy air, leaped, and came up smiling the straightest teeth in the world.

I followed him to the front lawn. When a car passed, he did a backflip and looked out the side of his eyes to see if any of the passengers were looking. Some pointed while others looked ahead dully at the road.

My cousin was a showoff, but I figured he was allowed the limelight before one appreciative dog who had come over to look. I envied him and his cloth gymnast shoes. I liked the way they looked, slim, black and cool. They seemed special, something I could never slip onto my feet.

I ate the plums and watched him until he was sweaty and out of breath. When he was finished, I begged him to let me wear his cloth shoes. Drops of sweat fell at his feet. He looked at me with disdain, ran a yellow towel across his face, and patted his neck dry. He tore the white tape from his wrists—I liked the tape as well and tried to paste it around my wrists. He washed off his hands. I asked him about the white powder, and he said it kept his hands dry. I asked him why he needed dry hands to do cartwheels and backflips. He said that all gymnasts kept their hands dry, then drank from a bottle of greenish water he said was filled with nutrients.

I asked him again if I could wear his shoes. He slipped them off and said, "OK, just for a while." The shoes were loose, but I liked them. I went to the front yard with my wrists dripping tape and my hands white as gloves. I smiled slyly and thought I looked neat. But when I did a cartwheel, the shoes flew off, along with the tape, and my cousin yelled and stomped the grass.

I was glad to get home. I was jealous and miserable, but the next day I found a pair of old vinyl slippers in the closet that were sort of like gymnastic shoes. I pushed my feet into them, tugging and wincing because they were too small. I took a few steps, admiring my feet, which looked like bloated water balloons, and went outside to do cartwheels on the front lawn. A friend skidded to a stop on his bike, one cheek fat with sunflower seeds. His mouth churned to a stop. He asked why I was wearing slippers on a hot day. I made a face at him and said that they were gymnastic shoes, not slippers. He watched me do cartwheels for a while, then rode away doing a wheelie.

I returned inside. I looked for tape to wrap my wrists, but could find only circle Band-Aids in the medicine cabinet. I dipped my hands in flour to keep them dry and went back outside to do cartwheels and, finally, after much hesitation, a backflip that nearly cost me my life when I landed on my head. I crawled to the shade, stars of pain pulsating in my shoulder and neck.

My brother glided by on his bike, smooth as a kite. He stared at me and asked why I was wearing slippers. I didn't answer him. My neck still hurt. He asked about the flour on my hands, and I told him to leave me alone. I turned on the hose and drank cool water.

I walked to Romain playground where I played Chinese checkers and was asked a dozen times why I was wearing slippers. I'm taking gymnastics, I lied, and these are the kind of shoes you wear. When one kid asked why I had white powder on my hands and in my hair, I gave up on Chinese checkers and returned home, my feet throbbing. But before I went inside, I took off the slippers. My toes cooled on the summery grass. I ran a garden hose on my feet and bluish ankles, and a chill ran up my back.

Dinner was a ten-minute affair of piranha-like eating and thirty minutes of washing dishes. Once finished, I returned to the backyard, where I again stuffed my feet into the slippers and did cartwheels by the dizzy dozens. After a while they were easy. I had to move on. I sucked in the summer air, along with the smoke of a faraway barbecue, and tried a backflip. I landed on my neck again, and this time I saw an orange burst behind my eyes. I lay on the grass, tired and sweaty, my feet squeezed in the vise of cruel slippers.

I watched the dusk settle and the first stars, pinpoints of unfortunate light tangled in telephone wires. I ate a plum, cussed, and pictured my cousin, who was probably cartwheeling to the audience of one sleeping dog.

THE PROMISES

I promised to rake the leaves and gather the tools from the lawn before it rained. I promised to make my bed. I promised to replace the cap to the toothpaste and wipe the sink of water spots and renegade hairs. I promised to stomp on the oil-spotted bags of garbage when our can was overflowing and ready to burst terrible gases. When my mother spoke, I said yes. When my stepfather spoke, I said yes, right now, and searched for the nearest broom. When an ambulance passed, I crossed myself in the name of the Father, the Son, and the Holy Ghost.

Promise. That's what Monsignor asked on the last day of school when he pressed papers into my hands and said that I should think of others. A dusty wind fluttered the school roll-up shades of St. John's Elementary. Sister Marie cast a meager shadow when she floated down the hallway. The picture of Jesus, flame to his brow, followed me out of the classroom and into the sunlight where my brother hid behind a corner with his crumpled report card.

I seemed pretty holy, inside and out, and to keep myself under control I promised to stay away from my older brother. Still, when he threw his report card at my face, I chased him around the card, tripped, and scuffed a knee and raked my palms against asphalt. My brother laughed, spit, and ran away without his books.

That was the beginning of summer. The heat was already yellow and fierce. I tried to be good. I played with my little brother who was bored of Tinkertoys and mud. I did the dishes without my mother's asking. I ran a finger across our furniture, collecting dust that I wiped on my jeans. I read three pages a day, prayed for the sick and the lost, and on Sundays lit puddly candles at my own expense. I promised myself to keep my drawer tidy, the balled socks in one corner, and the folded T-shirts in another.

But my older brother kept me from being good. One day at Romain playground, while I was busy with a craft project that would transform a toilet roll into a pencil holder, he came from behind and yanked off my special smoke-tinted glasses. Earlier in the week, a doctor had prescribed those glasses to wear because I had infected my eyes when I stared half a day into a box fan. It was a contest among the idiot boys of the block to see who could stare the longest. I won by more than an hour.

My brother stole my glasses and ran off, which sent me home walking like a blind man in the harsh Fresno sun. When Mother found out, she whipped my brother from one corner of the backyard to the other while I watched from the bedroom window. I adjusted my smoke-tinted glasses and sipped from my Tupperware cup of Kool-Aid. That night in our bunk beds, my brother promised to get me back. I laughed at my brother, but in the dark of poor vision I was scared. The next day I returned to the playground to finish my toilet-roll pencil holder and start on a planter. From the garbage I had pulled a Campbell's soup can, splashed it with peat moss, and painted it red. I glued on bottle caps I had dug out with a spoon from a gas station Coke machine: one row of Coca-Cola caps, then a row of Orange Crush, and finally one of Dr Pepper. When I finished with this detail, I packed dirt into the can, poked in two pinto beans, and watered them carefully so the bottle caps wouldn't get wet and fall off.

I was pleased with my planter. When Mother came home that afternoon from candling eggs for Safeway, I took her by the hand to the backyard to show her. "Very pretty," she said, her face unmoved. I showed my baby brother whom I had to boost into my arms. My sister seemed mildly interested. My older brother popped his fist into a baseball mitt and spit.

I intended to enter my planter into the crafts contest at the playground. I also intended to enter my pencil holder, my lanyard dog chain, my plaster-of-Paris footprint of Baby Brother, and my pickle-jar vase decorated with spray-painted macaroni. But my real hope was on the planter. For a week I watered it faithfully as I waited for the beans to unfurl from the earth. Each day I sat in the sunlight, reading books and occasionally smiling at my plant. I reglued the bottle caps that fell off, whisked away ants that came to tunnel holes in the dirt, and watered the beans which in my mind would soon push skywards and beyond.

Five days went by and I began to worry. I poured more and more water into the can, but nothing seemed to happen. I spoke to it softly, and muttered prayers. I moved it into the shade, thinking perhaps that it was thirsty for shadow. Finally, on the day of judging, I gathered my projects, including my planted can of dirt, and carried them to the playground. When I returned home I prayed and remembered my promises of dishes, dust, and tidy drawers. I did my chores, and mowed the lawn with a rusty mower.

The next day when I returned to Romain playground, I was a winner! My lanyard and plaster-of-Paris footprint took second place. My toilet-roll pencil holder won third, and my planter, minus its green growth, received fourth. In celebration, the coach poured us paper cups of Coca-Cola and handed out fistfuls of popcorn and candy.

When the party was over, my sister and I bal-
anced our crafts in our arms and returned home.
Debra had won two first place certificates and
bragged all the way home and into autumn. Still, I
was happy and taped my certificates on my bedroom wall. That evening after dinner I took my
planter to the front yard where I sat on the lawn
sucking a blade of grass and wondering why the
plants had not come up. My brother Rick rode by
on his bike and yelled, "I told you I'd get you." I
looked up at him as he rode off, and then looked at
the can. I scratched the surface of the dirt lightly
and then dug with the full force of my fingernails.
Nothing. The beans were gone.

I looked up from the can and, with moist lips,
muttered a promise, "My brother has to die."

THE LOCKET

I never liked jewelry. My sister Debra did. Twenty
Bazooka comic strips and a dollar—after a three-
week binge of reading teenage romances while
waiting for the mailman—brought her a gold-
painted locket, studded with plastic pearls and a
fake diamond. I wanted her to choose the minia-
ture binoculars because I helped her chew at least
seven pieces of pink bubble gum and gave her a
clean dime in exchange for our once-a-week pudding dessert. We were always selling desserts to

each other. We were always short a dime or a quarter, and our only bargaining chip was dessert, especially the pudding mother served in gold-rimmed goblets, the kind kings and queens used in Robin Hood movies.

I wanted Debra to choose the binoculars. My head was large, but my eyes were small as a cat's, maybe even smaller. I could look through both lenses with one eye, and what I wanted was a better look at our neighbor, a junior college student who swam in an aluminum-sided Doughboy pool. She used a ladder to get in, and often just stood on the ladder fiddling with her top and snapping her bikini bottom back into place. I could spy on her from behind our fence, the binoculars to my right eye because that one seemed to work better.

But Debra chose the locket. When it arrived in a business-sized envelope, I waved it at her and said, "It's here." Angrily, she snatched it from me and took it to her room. I ate an afternoon bowl of Cocoa Puffs and watched a movie about giant ants no flame thrower could stop. I looked at her bedroom door now and then, wondering what was going on. Later, just before the ants got fried with a laser, she came out stinking of perfume, the locket around her brown neck. She didn't look at me as she went out the front door and crossed the street to see her friend, Jill.

My sister was eleven. She still clacked the plastic faces of Barbie and Ken together, made them hug, made them cry and run back to each other, stiff arms extended, faces wet with pretend tears from the bathroom sink. But she and Jill played with them less and less. Now they were going for the real thing: boys with washed faces.

In spite of the plastic pearls and the chip of glass centered in the middle, the locket made her look grown-up. I didn't tease her, and she didn't tease me about wearing rummage-sale baseball cleats.

All summer Debra wore the locket, and Jill wore one, too, an expensive one her mother had bought at Penney's. But Debra didn't care. She loved the locket whose metal chain left her neck green. Mother admired the locket, said it made her look elegant. That summer, Debra began to complain less and less about doing the dishes.

When a pearl fell out, she glued it back in. Another lost its grip and rolled into the floor furnace. She vacuumed the furnace of its ghostly lint, and shook out the bag and ran her fingers through the stinking hair, lint, broken potato chips, Cocoa Puffs, Cheerios, staples, bits of Kleenex, dead ants, and blue, flowery marble. She searched through the debris until, miraculously, she found the tiny pearl. She glued it back into place and gave her locket a rest.

One day, while Debra was at the playground swimming, I snuck into her bedroom to peek in the locket because I knew she kept something in the frame. She was always snapping it open and closed, always feeling pretty happy when she looked down at her breasts, twin mounds that had begun to cast small shadows. When I opened it, slowly because the clasp looked fragile, I saw a face that was mostly an eyeball looking at me. I stared back at the eyeball, and after a moment realized that it was Paul of The Beatles. It was Paul's eyeball, a bit droopy, a bit sad like his songs. Paul was favored by the girls who rode their bikes up and down the block singing "Michelle, ma belle."

A few days later I checked the locket again. Paul's eyeball was gone, and now I was staring at a smiling Herman and the Hermits. Herman looked happy. His hair was long and soft, and his teeth were large and charmingly crooked. I smiled wide and thought for a moment that I looked like Herman. A few days later it was back to Paul in a new picture that she had cut out of a magazine. I thumbed through the magazine, emptied of all the famous pop stars, and looked around the room. Almost everything was pink. The furry rug, the canopy bed, the bottles of perfume and nail polish, the much-hugged pillow, everything except the chest of drawers which she intended to paint by fall. I left in a hurry when I heard Debra's bike skid to a halt in the driveway.

All summer it was Paul's eyeball, Herman's teeth, and one time Paul Revere with his colonial hat. Debra began to polish her nails and walk more slowly, erect as a ladder. By fall, the chest of drawers was pink and Mother was no longer worried about the green around her neck where the chain rested—an allergic reaction to cheap metal. Debra no longer wore the locket. She was saving Bazooka comics for a camera that came with a free

roll of film. She had her first boyfriend and wanted
to take his picture on the sly, wanted more than a
droopy eyeball or toothy smile. She wanted the
entire face, and some of the neck.

PART THREE

THE HERO

Tony was handsome and so strong that I stood next to him when baseball teams were chosen. I was picked third from the last, right before the kid with the eyeglasses taped together at the bridge, right before the fat kid with a river of blue veins on his belly.

A slow pitch over the plate was nothing to Tony. The mousy scurry of a ball between short and third was nothing. A pop-up in a glaring sky was nothing. Tony was quick, fair when fights broke out, and the nickel in his pocket was yours if you asked. I kept my mouth busy with sunflower seeds, my fist popping in my mitt's pocket.

I sat on a splintery bench those long innings while both teams scored a dozen runs. I clawed the chain link fence while everyone else became a hero. Their eyelids stung from the dust of sliding into second. Their hands were sweaty from standing in the outfield and pounding their gloves waiting for the ball to sail off a bad pitch. When a pitch connected on the wrong part of the bat an electric shock ran up their arms and died at the elbow. They were lucky to have these feelings.

But I had my turn. I reached third base five times that summer and scored once when the wind peeled dirt around the plate, and the catcher, the boy with blue veins on his belly, couldn't see. The reason I made home, they said, was because I was skinny. I blended with the light, blended with the sand around the plate. Once, when I was hit in the back on a bad pitch, my teammates huddled over and begged Tony to let them take my place. Tony brought me to my feet by saying, "Try again."

Maybe Tony was smart. I don't know. But he was the first poet I knew. He thought a lot about life after childhood. Sitting on his lawn, he worried about the air. He said the mountains should be right there, and his finger was God's finger touching Adam's. I looked where he pointed and knew what he meant. After a rain storm, the air cleared and we had a chance to start over, to park every car for good and walk, to shut the factories down and feed ourselves more on prayer than red meat.

We rode our bikes to the country thinking that nature began where the stoplights gave way to stop signs, and trucks outnumbered cars. We looked at cows, and neither of us was disturbed that flies crawled over their faces. Even the stink of the chicken hatchery was nature. We rode until we came to a dairy, where we each drank a quart of chocolate milk and then relieved ourselves on a patch of collapsed mushrooms. We sat in the grass of a quiet roadside, looking west where the moun-

tains rose in a blue haze. Jays maddened the air
with their bickering. The wind moved the shadows of the oak trees, and a chill ran along our arms.

Tony, a stalk of sweet grass in his mouth, asked
what I wanted to do with my life. I didn't have to
think twice. I said I wanted to join the army so that
I could travel. He pulled the grass from his mouth,
and said he used to have the same wish but now he
wanted to take the bullet for the president.

I looked at him, confused. "What do you mean?"

"I mean, I want to die for the president. Like
President Kennedy. But it's too late for him."

I pictured my grandmother's living room where
portraits of President Kennedy and Jesus with
flame over his brow hung on the wall.

Tony explained that someone had to step in
front of gunfire for the president, that it might as
well be him. He wasn't happy all the time, and he
had dreams about water that kept him from a
good night's sleep. In the summer light, his eyes
didn't look puffy. They were clear in the corners.
He did seem quiet, though, and he had gone from
swimming at the playground pool to playing chess
under a tree.

"Don't you think it would hurt?" I asked.

He looked at the mountains for a long time. I
followed his stare to a hawk floating on warm air. A
passing truck made him wake up and say,
"Maybe."

The ride back home was slower, less fun, though
we did stop at a canal to walk in murky water
flowing west toward a stand of sunlit eucalyptus.

We sat on the bank and chewed sweet grass, the sun flaring when the branches moved.

All summer I slept hard as a stone, and only during a dumb, playground fist fight did I think about the bullet Tony would someday take. Summer was baseball, and the wish to hit someone home. Summer was a stalk of grass hanging from a mouth.

Like other heroes, Tony moved away. He left without a goodbye. I peeked in his front window and saw a cardboard box of old clothes, an ironing board leaning against the wall, and yellow curtains crumpled on the floor. A bare light bulb burned in the kitchen. I went around to the back, where I lit a leaf fire and thought about the zero a bullet makes in flesh. The sky was gray. Faraway birds were migrating. The orange tree was turning orange, bobbing the perpetual fruit of all that comes back.

THE BEATLES

It was scary at home. After Father died, after two years and many months, my mother remarried. The man who showed up with boxes of clothes sat in our only good chair, drank, and looked at a television screen with a flickering line through its middle. He never laughed at Jackie Gleason's bug-eyed jokes, Red Skelton's hobo walk, or Lucille

Ball's bosom bulging a hundred chicken eggs. He just looked, crushed beer cans, and moved the box fan in his direction, the blades like a thousand spoons. His stiff hair, which was hard from a yellow paste in a jar, didn't move, but the lapels of his work shirt flapped in the breeze.

I stayed outside a lot. It was scary to go inside, and besides, friends were sitting on their front lawns singing Beatle songs. Cathy was very good. She could start off humming "I Want to Hold Your Hand," and because she was older, in junior high, sing the words without feeling embarrassed. Her body rocked, yellow hair bouncing and perfuming the air about us, and her mouth made a near perfect "O" when her voice lifted on the word "hold." At first, I didn't join her or the others, but when I saw my sister start singing, her words dragging softly behind Cathy's, I started singing too, but stopped just before the song came to an end.

I was too shy to sing on the front lawn because my voice was flat, and I was scared that my friends riding by on bicycles would make fun of me. But they just rode by, squeezing bags of sunflower seeds, their mitts hanging on the handlebars. They wanted to join us, but didn't know how.

David and I saved enough money from mowing lawns to buy a tape recorder from Long's Drugs. We wanted to hear our voices, to sing along with Beatle records. "I Want to Hold Your Hand" was already off the charts, but we still liked it, that one and "Love, Love Me Do."

That winter we sang in David's bedroom because it was too scary at my house. My stepfather didn't like The Beatles because they were like girls, he said. He crushed a can and asked if we wanted to grow up queer. We shook our heads no. He turned his liquid gaze to the TV, the line cutting deeper into the screen, and we lowered our faces into our school work.

On Saturday, I cut my hair to please him, a butch that showed that my scalp was blue under my black hair. But still he grumbled when The Beatles appeared on Ed Sullivan, right after Señor Wences, who made his money by dabbing lipstick on his fist and making it open and close like lips. "Sí," the fist said, "Sí, I drink the water." My stepfather stared at the fist, which was dressed in a tiny wig. When The Beatles came on, John running onto the stage so that his hair bounced, my stepfather made a face and changed the channel. He crushed a can, and we, brother and sister, left the room to fill in dot-to-dot cartoons at the kitchen table.

Because David paid two dollars more for the tape recorder and bought the batteries, he got to be Paul all the time, Paul, the cute Beatle with sad eyes. I had to be George and wasn't allowed to beat pencils against David's makeshift drum set of two shoe boxes and one oatmeal box.

Neither cared what the other looked like when we jumped around singing "Love, Love Me Do." David's beagle, which looked like Ringo with his mouth closed, pawed the bedspread and licked himself. David's mother was too kind to bang on the door, and only now and then threw us outside to get fresh air. With the bedroom windows closed, we sweated and beat holes into our paper drums.

David had to cut his hair, too, because his father had bought him three fresh batteries. He had to stay on his good side because his father drank, too, and would sometimes stare at the sprinkler and become so self-absorbed that no one dared tell him that the water was flowing into the gutter.

One evening, David let me take the tape recorder home. When I walked in the front door, my mom and stepfather were arguing in the living room. The blades in the box fan were turning faster than I remembered, rattling the pages of our dot-to-dot magazines on the TV tray. I went to my bedroom without looking at them, closed the door, and recorded my stepfather: "My feet hurt. You don't give a shit when the car don't work. You'll never give a shit. I work all day and your kids aren't happy with food." My mother said: "You don't know a damn thing about my children. You've ruined the chair. Where were you when I told you to come home? You don't know a damn thing about anything. The cooler don't work. Damn fool, you got rice on your face."

While they went back and forth, I did a dot-to-dot cartoon, looking up now and then to stare into the mirror sadly because I didn't look anything like George of The Beatles. I would never be famous, never travel across the Atlantic Ocean, never pick up a guitar and have kids go crazy. When my parents stopped after the front door was opened and slammed shut, I played the argument back because I wanted to understand what they were saying and why they were so loud. They sounded scary. The batteries were weak, their voices slurred, and finally my mom's voice died on the word "face." It took more batteries to make me sing again.

THE BABYSITTER

When Frank, our babysitter from juvie, picked some black stuff from under his fingernail with a playing card and suggested that we take my mom's car (Mom was out dancing for the evening), I stopped marching around the living room with smashed Pepsi cans on the heels of my tennis shoes. I had never been in a car driven by someone who was only three years older than me, which is to say, a fifteen-year-old. Rick, my older brother, was camping in a friend's backyard, while Debra played on the couch with our baby brother.

"You don't know how to drive," I said, unhooking the Pepsi cans from my shoes. But I was eager to help drive the car. I had once started the car and revved it up until smoke filled the garage and the five kids sitting with me became sick. The mother of one of the other kids later called, and I was spanked from one corner of the room to the other. I thought of that day and shook my head. "Mom'll find out."

Frank fanned out a deck of cards on the kitchen table and asked, "How?"

"She just will."

He shuffled the cards and said, "Pick one."

I picked a card: a jack of clubs with a little spittle of plum on his chin. He reshuffled the deck, fanned out the cards again, and said, "Pick another."

It was the jack, with the glob of plum.

Frank got up from the table and dipped his pudgy fingers into the Disneyland coffee cup where the keys were kept. "Come on, don't be a baby." My baby brother looked up with spittle from thumb sucking hanging on his face. Debra got off the couch. "Mom's gonna get you if you drive her car."

"No, sir," I said. I looked up at Frank. "Will she?"

Frank said we could go for a short ride, and if we didn't tell he would buy us a milkshake. He said he was almost fifteen, and on farms people knew how to drive tractors when they were twelve. I said he didn't live on a farm, but he said that I was missing the point. He reminded us that he would buy us a shake, a jumbo one if we agreed. Debra looked at me, and I at her. That was enough for us, and we carried the baby into our Chevy, which was parked in the driveway. While we snuck into the car, ever mindful of the neighbors, Frank walked tall as a Marine and twirled the keychain on his index finger.

"Stay down," I warned Debra and my baby brother who were in the backseat on their knees.

Frank started the engine, adjusted the mirror and the seat, and said, "Here goes," not looking over his shoulder as he backed out of the driveway. I peeked out of the window like an alligator and saw Cross-Eyed Johnny shooting marbles in his driveway. A shirtless Mr. Prince was watering his yellow lawn. Mrs. Hancock was tying back a rose bush with strips of bedsheet.

The Chevy purred as it picked up speed, a tail of blue smoke trailing. When the car slowed to a stop at the end of the block, we sat up. Frank seemed in control. He looked both ways, then accelerated smoothly, warm wind filling the car and rattling the newspapers on the floorboard.

As we drove up a street past neighbors sitting in lawn chairs under the orange glow of porch lights, Debra said she wanted a banana shake. I thought chocolate would be fine, though banana would be OK as long as we had two straws to pump our cheeks full of sweetness. Our baby brother, who had yet to squeal more than "Mama" and "shasha," said nothing. He was pulling at the thread of a busted seam in the upholstery.

I noticed one of Frank's arms cocked on the window. I told him he had better drive with both hands, but he laughed and said driving was safer with one hand because the other hand was needed to signal for turns. He slouched down, and I said he should sit up so he could see more of the road. He laughed and said slouching was safer because if we got in a wreck his face wouldn't hit the windshield. Debra asked if we were going to get in a wreck, and he said, "Only if we stop." He ran a stop sign and laughed so that spittle flew from his mouth. It was then that I knew we had made a mistake getting in the car with him. He laughed and looked at us with his eyes closed. He laughed and wriggled the steering wheel so that the car shimmied. He laughed and took both hands off the wheel. He laughed when the car veered toward the gutter and leaves exploded into the air. I socked him in the arm, hard, and told him he had better drive right, or else.

Frank's laughter wound down to a giggle. "OK," he said. He turned onto Belmont Avenue and as we approached the Starlight burger stand, he said, "Is that where you want to get your milkshakes?"

"Yeah, that's it," we screamed. Our baby brother got up on his knees to look. A silvery thread hung from his wet mouth.

The car got closer and closer, and Frank repeated, "Is that it, that one?"

"Yeah," we screamed again.

"That one," he repeated, "that one?"

Yeah, yeah, yeah.

Frank laughed and passed up the burger stand. "Oops, we missed it."

We sat back down, feeling cheated. The air about us stank of burgers.

Frank made a reckless U-turn that made the tires squeal, and our baby brother rolled over like a sack of groceries. I socked Frank in the arm and warned him that he had better drive right. He said "OK, OK, all right already." He smirked, then smiled a large, idiot grin as we approached the burger stand we had just passed. He pointed again and asked: "That one?"

Debra and I leaned our faces into the open window, warm air gushing into our mouths. "Yeah, that one."

"That one?" Frank kidded.

"Yeah, that one," we screamed a little louder.

The Chevy slowed but didn't stop. I saw a kid about my age, cheeks collapsed, sucking on a milk-shake, and a baby in a stroller feeding on a spoon-ful of ice cream. At a redwood table, a family of four was biting into their burgers at the same time. Mad, I climbed into the backseat. Debra and I grumbled and crossed our arms. Our baby brother played with strings of his spittle. He smiled at me, and I could see real string looped on the back of his mouth. Grimacing, I scraped his tongue of string and a milky paste.

I turned back to Frank. "You're a liar," I said, trying to hurt his feelings. "You were a liar before you were born!"

Frank laughed and said, "No, the car just didn't stop. I think something's wrong with the brakes." He scared his face into lines and bugged out his eyes. He shielded his face with his arms and screamed, "Look out! Look out!" as we came to a red light. The Chevy groaned to a halt, and he turned around, with one arm on the seat, and said, "I guess the brakes fixed themselves."

Frank punched the gas pedal and the Chevy coughed and jerked forward while our heads jerked back. Baby brother rolled over one more time, fingers in his mouth.

"We wanna get out, right now!" I said. "I mean it!"

"I'm going to tell Mom," Debra threatened.

Frank looked into the rear view mirror with closed eyes. "Wanna get out? Good idea." He opened the door and stuck one foot out. I saw the rush of asphalt, some burger stand litter, and one poor sparrow flattened to an oily shadow.

"You better drive us back home, right now," Debra said. "I mean it!"

"Right now? No, we're gonna get a milkshake." He closed the door and did a U-turn. We looked ahead: the burger stand's neon was fluttering, saying BU G RS FOR YO . There were two cars and people ordering under a stinky fan. Music was blaring from a loudspeaker.

We began to smell burgers, and I could hear the slurp of a drained Coke. Frank pointed and asked, "That one? That one right there?"

We looked but didn't say anything. I was wondering if Rick and I could beat him up. Debra could help out, and maybe we could pin him to the floor and let baby brother drool on his face. Maybe when we got home Mom would be standing in the front window with a belt in her hands. I figured that Frank would get the first spanking, and then Mom would be too tired to spank us that hard. She might not even spank us at all, only make us do the dishes until we moved out of the house.

Only after baby brother messed his plastic pants, and Debra and I yanked together on Frank's hair so that a muscle in his neck popped, did we return to our street and the sound of hiss-

ing sprinklers in the summer dark. We slammed
the car door, cussed, and stomped into the house
with a smirking Frank offering apologies. We
changed baby brother, who squealed and bit more
holes into his rubber rattler. Debra and I picked
up a bundle of crayons and sat down at the kitchen
table. Frank shuffled the cards, played game after
game of solitaire, cheating each time, and then
asked as he got up to fix a pitcher of purple Kool-
Aid, "Whatta you guys wanna do?"

THE STRAY

Stray dogs came with the rain. I found them at
the garbage can, paws up, lapping egg shells and
milk cartons, chomping yellow rinds of fat. When I
whistled "Here boy" and snapped a finger, they
turned to look at me. Their eyes were the eyes of
sad mules. Their lolling tongues were barely pink.
They looked thin in a coat of rain on bony shoulders. The rain came and went, and the dogs followed through the puddles.

Dogs of childhood. Once, after a scolding from
my mother, I walked down an alley stomping rain
puddles and kicking rickety fences. No one under-
stood me. I turned over a garbage can and
brooded until I was a mile from home and the sun,
yellow as a vase of flowers, broke through the
clouds. Slim fingers of steam wavered off the

fences. Puddles reflected the rush of white clouds and the wind picked up the scent of washed blossoms. Some old mother taking out the garbage waved at me, and I waved back stiffly. Still, I was lonely. I wanted to run away, but didn't know how. Should I return home for my toothbrush and a change of clothes? Should I steal a dollar from Mom's purse and take a bus to the outskirts of town?

A stray dog looked up from feasting on the guts of a swollen garbage can. His tail wagged twice, and he rolled a tongue over shiny teeth. When I called him, he joined my side, his paws clicking against the ground, our breaths white in the cold.

We walked for a good mile, each of us dragging a sled of loneliness. We walked through a puddle, breaking the mirror of its surface. When the dog barked at a squirrel clawing up a tree, I barked too, and felt better. I helped the dog climb onto the hood of an abandoned car and told him about myself. I told him that my father was dead, that I didn't like home, that I was terrible at numbers. I told him that I had seen the sea once and loved it more than snow. I wanted to live near the coast, I told him. The trees were bent from wind, but the people walked straight up, happy to be near the crash of gray-white waves. I told him I thought about God, and that the statue of the Lord in our bedroom glowed when the lights went out.

But I could only say so much to a dog. It was better to touch. I ran a hand through his damp fur and scratched him behind his neck until he nearly fell asleep. His body was warm, and his shoulders stuck through his fur like wings. He breathed in hard puffs through a black, Tinkertoy nose. His ears were as soft as worn wallets.

I felt better. The sun slid behind a cloud, chilling the autumn air. I shivered and jumped from the car. The dog followed me up the alley, my strides now longer and my face open to wind and a silver mist. I tugged three oranges from a rain-glistening tree. Two went into the pocket of my jacket, and the other one I peeled, offering a slice to the dog, who snapped at it gently and held it in his mouth like a fang. He let it drop to the muddy ground, and I knew that this dog lived for meat. At a garbage can, I picked through soggy paper bags for bones and leftovers, any treasure I could spill into a pie tin. I dug past the light bulbs and egg cartons, past tuna cans and a mountain of coffee grinds. I flicked ants from my hands. I dug until I found a ham bone nearly the size of a baseball bat.

Stray dogs should live with human names. That day, I called him Charlie, but I could have called him Sam or Pete. I said, "Charlie," and he looked up from his bone, a shred of meat hanging from his mouth. He licked his lips and lowered his face. His teeth clacked, and his tongue rolled over the best parts.

"Charlie," I said, and he looked up. "Charlie," I called once more. He looked up, this time whining and pumping his wet paws.

I dug my fingers into another orange and unraveled the skin in one piece. I ate standing in a rain puddle that reflected the bunched clouds and a tangle of telephone wires. It showed me, too, or most of me. My face was round, and my teeth were like long candles when I smiled. I smiled and picked at a piece of orange wedged between my front teeth.

I left Charlie and walked in the direction of kids playing front-yard football. They grunted to take each other down, fumbled catches, and snapped the ball on the wrong count. I watched them argue over a catch, then watched a player fall and shout that the other team was cheating.

I returned home to find my mother at the kitchen table bending over the sewing machine, her mouth shut tight on three needles. A bell of warmth rose from the floor furnace. I sat near the front window, tired but happier than when I left the house.

The next morning I found a stray near our garbage can. I called, "Hey, Charlie," and he looked up with rain on his face.

THE WEATHER

January doesn't show its true face until you can scratch a cold window with a finger. As a kid I drew faces and looked out to the street through the eyeholes. I saw cars shrouded white with frost, gray gutters, and trees stiff with brown sparrows huddled on black boughs. I didn't like the cold much. It kept me inside, bored in every bone, because Mother believed that a cold or a flu lurked in the wind. Sometimes when we were outside and a wind was passing, she would make us stop in our tracks and tell us to hold our breath. Wind carried pollen and disease, a whip of dust that could hurt an eye. Wind carried omens and rumor, insects with multiple pincers, and chemical smells of faraway dumps.

Wind was one thing, frost another. I walked on hard lawns and looked back, happy that my shoe prints were visible, that a dog would stop and sniff them. I followed bike tracks and got nowhere. I followed clouds as well, the heavy machinery of rain that did more than keep me inside. It made my brother and me fight a lot, made my mother sit at the table stirring black-black coffee, the worry of bills resting on a sharp elbow. On those days I tried to stay quiet by rearranging my sock drawer. I owned a lot of mismatched socks, but blue was almost like black, and I figured with long pants no one would know the difference. With my gym socks, all white, it was an easy task, but more difficult to juggle. Three in the air, and every one of them coming down like snowballs.

Rain weeped on the kitchen window. Rain dripped like tears in our almond and plum trees. Spider skeins glistened and stray dogs working on three legs and two bitten ears showed up at the garbage cans. After the rain, puddles marked the world's dents. I enjoyed jumping puddles and riding a slow bike through deep puddles that welled at the end of our block. The gutters carried silt and gum wrappers, but when the sun came out, the rivers slowed and eventually came to a muddy stop. The fences steamed and an armada of snails, antennae up, crawled across the cement walk.

Hail spooked me. Just as I was ready to bite into a peanut butter sandwich, hail ticked the front window. I put the sandwich aside, and all of us poked our faces at the window. Hail bounced like popcorn on the lawn, and my brother, a big fool who would try anything, ran outside and danced under the hail, mouth open but eyes closed. The hail tasted faintly of metal when I licked a handful, and the pellets dissolved like a squashed bug between my thumb and index finger.

Hail wasn't much good for show-and-tell, but a branch struck by lightning made some of the students perk up when I told my class, "This branch got it, and if I was in the tree I would have got it, too." I dragged it back home afterwards and let it fall in the backyard. Three foolish sparrows immediately jumped on and fluttered their wings.

Snow didn't come our way. We lived in a valley, but if I stood on a fence I could see the Sierras, their caps tipped white. Once, though, snow, like torn-up homework, fell and made everyone come outside to hold out their hands and tongues. The town was happy for ten minutes, and when the snow stopped and the white dissolved into the lawns, we all went inside.

Tornados were just pictures in a book, a disaster headline in the newspaper, or scenes in the movie *The Wizard of Oz.* But once, a tall, elevator shaft of dust whirls passed through our playground. My friend Victor tried to jump inside it, and was momentarily blinded by dust. We cheered for more destruction. The chewing gum was ripped from my sister's mouth. Cut grass crowned our hair and stuck to the back of our sticky necks. The dust whirl cut through a chain link fence, carrying away leaves, candy wrappers and kids who followed it for miles.

The sun gave us another kind of weather. In summer, the heat made you think twice about going outside. The asphalt softened, the lawns grew spidery brown, and the dogs crept like shadows. Chickens sometimes fell over, and June bugs hissed on the screen door, wanting in. A girl on our block had a three-foot pool, and although she wouldn't let boys swim, we were permitted to watch her and her girlfriends churn the water white and chant, "We're the queen of the surfers." We sat in the mulberry tree, hot in the face and wet in every crevice.

With nightfall came stars, and with the stars, the quiet of sitting on a front lawn. TVs showed through the windows, blue as heaven. From dark porches, cigarettes glowed. The littlest of the kids made sparks by scratching a screwdriver across the cement. Teenagers sat on car fenders, socking each other in the arm. I lay on my back, the coolness of the lawn pricking my neck and arms. Summer was like winter, only different in degrees.

THE CANAL

The canal raced out of town before us, green sparkling water with leaves carrying troubled ants and the microscopic makings of boredom. The sun flashed off the surface, and wind brushed tiers of weeds along the bank. My best friend and I sat at the bank, desperate because no girls bothered to turn red when we were around. They chewed gum and pressed transistor radios to their ears. They turned the pages of their magazines, brushing back their hair with hands that were white doves.

We poured sand through our fingers and wondered out loud how the first-period coach could get so mean by 8:30. We were no good at long-distance running and had to hold our sides when we ran laps. The coach's silver whistle filled with saliva, anger, and milkish hate.

"Hell's bells," he yelled, clipboard in hand. His stomach was an imperfect ball, and his cap said "Coach." Even in the morning, faint moons of sweat hung under his arms. We ran because we didn't know any better, and played volleyball because it was spring and it was all right to show our legs. We jumped a few times, but mostly we argued about the rules, then showered, left school by the south gate, and drove to the canal. We didn't know rivers or lakes, and the sea was a postcard that came our way now and then. The pond water at Roeding Park Zoo was dead to life, except mosquitoes gorged on the blood of dogs and half-naked kids.

The canal water was swift under the afternoon sun, but cold as a frozen spoon. We sat in loose sand and talked about the coach, our step-fathers slouching in their sour chairs in front of the TV, and (if we had the money) the record albums we would buy by T-Rex and Hendrix. Their music was spooky, especially T-Rex with their faraway planet music, and their album covers held a wisdom of psychedelic meaning that would render us intelligent if we looked at them long enough.

We tossed rocks into the water and thought about how earlier in the week we had parked in front of our teacher's house. We both loved Mrs. Tuttle, the blue of her inner thighs, her laugh, her hair teased by wind and hair spray. We knew it was wrong to look up her address at a filthy gas station and drive by, late, with only the parking lights on. We knew it was wrong to return the following night and park in front of her house and watch the bluish light of TV fill her drapes. We imagined her husband sitting in a La-Z-Boy recliner, and imagined Mrs. Tuttle's knitting needles clicking in her lap. We had wild thoughts about the two of them squeezed together as they sat side by side like pals. When we couldn't stand it any longer, we started the car and drove to the canal to watch the pulsating stars on the water. The radio grinned an orange light, and we tried our best to make out the words to a loud song.

We walked along the canal, shivering, until we came to a cluster of mobile homes. At one, the TV blared. Wind banged the gate, and a sickish porch-light outlined the frame of a swing set. A black rope hung from a tree. We climbed over a wire fence and hung on that rope, swung, and laughed because it was something to do. When a dog began to bark, we made our way back to the car where we sat waiting for the radio to play T-Rex. Mostly the radio sold cars and couches, but now and then a planet-music song would play and make us think that we were not going to live very long.

We drove to town, and for the rest of the night we took corners sharply, snickering when the tires squealed and sticky Coke bottles rolled and clinked on the floorboard. At yellow-lights-going-red, we braked as hard as we could without dying.

That was earlier in the week. Now it was Friday, late afternoon, and we were so lonely we were talking about parents. We didn't understand them. They liked us best when we had rakes in our hands and a slave's smile as we hauled a burlap sack of grass clippings over our shoulders. Or when orange soap suds climbed our elbows as we scrubbed a pan of hardened macaroni and cheese. We talked about the coach, grades, and Mr. Moss, the biology teacher, and how he made the prettiest girl in class kiss a petri dish. Three days later, a horrible fungus had climbed up the sides, ready to spread into the hallway.

We huddled in our jackets. Our companions were bickering jays in the bush and a bloated frog flopping in the weeds. We looked east, where the

Sierras were still white with snow, and west, where the wind peeled up dry earth from foreclosed farms. We could go only so far in our car but, while we sat, the canal water got the hell out of town.

THE NILE

By seventh grade I knew better than to spit while girls were around. I had started liking them and those little bumps behind their blouses. Their legs were still stork-thin, but they were looking better all the time.

I no longer acted dumb. I swallowed that lump of spit that formed in P.E., feigned a smile, and walked around looking troubled because everyone had begun to perceive me as a thinker. I looked moody, but inside I was wildly happy. I was getting good grades by simply sitting up in my chair and folding my hands on the desk. The nuns were right after all. Posture could get you anywhere. Now that I was going to public school, I was in the front row studying the Euphrates.

First impressions mattered a lot. My friend, Cesar, threw up eggs in civics, and because it smelled bad and lingered in the air like mustard gas, no one liked him for three years. I felt sorry for Cesar, and for nerdy classmates who didn't catch on that it was insane to drink at the water fountain near west hall. That was where stray dogs lapped water. Everyone knew that, even the teachers who drank from red Thermos cups. Everyone except the dips and nerds.

When I was with a girl, say Rita Castro, who used to share her homework with me, I was always careful to close my mouth after I had said something. I thought it was impolite to let your mouth hang open. Who wanted to look at a tongue, or crooked teeth? I was also scared that a gnat might fly into my mouth and I would choke and throw up just as some good-looking girls came into the library. After that, I would have to hang out with Cesar, who spent his recess near the backstop with three fat boys.

I began to think that mother was right when she said good manners were important. I began to say "yes," not "uh-huh," and began to walk, not run when someone called. When my aunts kissed me on the cheek, I didn't turn away and make a sour face. When my uncles after a drinking binge dropped on the front lawn, I no longer rained flakes of grass on their heads. Instead, I peeled an orange and listened to them mumble about their lives.

One afternoon my friend Scott and I got it into our heads that girls liked having their pictures taken. With a borrowed camera, we went downtown. We didn't have film, but we thought we looked pretty smart kneeling, one eye squinted, before a rose bush and snapping the shutter a hundred times. Rose bushes were one thing, girls another. When we clicked the camera at them, they hid their faces in sweaters, giggled, and ran. We enjoyed seeing them run, skirts jumping above their knees.

One time we ran after them, laughing with our mouths open. Then they stopped, and we freaked out. We had to say something, and I was so scared, so shy, that I blurted out that my pants cost $7.95. Red climbed to my face, and I ran away, thinking that maybe that's how Cesar felt when eggs exploded from his mouth.

Neither Scott nor I was good at math. The girls knew this, and fanned themselves with their B+ quizzes. I was good at geography, though. Mr. Johnson pointed to a map of Africa and baffled everyone by saying that the Nile flowed northward. It looked impossible because, according to the map, the river flowed *up*, and every other river in the world flowed *down*.

"Water can't do that," a girl remarked. Some boys shook their heads. I raised a hand and explained that Africa was mostly rocks and sand and what looked like a flat surface on the map was really mountains. Of course, when I said this, my posture was straight and my hands were folded coolly on the desk. The teacher, Mr. Johnson, wiped his hands clean of chalk dust and smiled.

I was happy after figuring out the Nile River, and during lunch, Scott and I walked around the schoolyard taking pictures. We clicked some pigeons eating toast. We clicked a bicycle seat puddled with rain. The clouds, pulled thin above the trees, seemed interesting as well.

When three girls started following us, we pretended not to notice them. We busied our faces with deep thoughts and clicked a backstop scrawled with orange graffiti. The girls watched us a while, then left. We didn't see them again, up close that is, until we were at a ninth-grade dance. The one with piled hair now had short hair like a boy's. She and I danced and drank punch thick with round ice cubes. Toward the end of the evening we escaped to the parking lot. A sweep of headlights lit up her eyes. I kissed her and left moisture on her neck. She kissed me back, and told me about her family and her runaway brother. Her father was redfaced from welding, and her mother jittery from flailing her hands on a stenograph machine.

I said "yes" a couple of times with throaty conviction and asked her if she remembered how in geography I figured out why the Nile flowed *up*, not *down*. I told her that I was still good at geography and that I was getting good at words. I left more moisture on her neck and then breathed, "You *exude* feelings that remind me of Istanbul."

I perfumed the air with more beauty, then called it a night with a long, long kiss.

THE DRIVE-IN MOVIES

For our family, moviegoing was rare. But if our mom, tired from a week of candling eggs, woke up happy on a Saturday morning, there was a chance we might later scramble to our blue Chevy and beat nightfall to the Starlight Drive-In. My brother and sister knew this. I knew this. So on Saturday we tried to be good. We sat in the cool shadows of the TV with the volume low and watched cartoons, a prelude of what was to come.

One Saturday I decided to be extra good. When she came out of the bedroom tying her robe, she yawned a hat-sized yawn and blinked red eyes at the weak brew of coffee I had fixed for her. I made her toast with strawberry jam spread to all the corners and set the three boxes of cereal in front of her. If she didn't care to eat cereal, she could always look at the back of the boxes as she drank her coffee.

I went outside. The lawn was tall but too wet with dew to mow. I picked up a trowel and began to weed the flower bed. The weeds were really bermuda grass, long stringers that ran finger-deep in the ground. I got to work quickly and in no time crescents of earth began rising under my finger-nails. I was sweaty hot. My knees hurt from kneel-ing, and my brain was dull from making the trowel go up and down, dribbling crumbs of earth. I dug for half an hour, then stopped to play with the neighbor's dog and pop ticks from his poor snout.

I then mowed the lawn, which was still beaded with dew and noisy with bees hovering over clover. This job was less dull because as I pushed the mower over the shaggy lawn, I could see it looked tidier. My brother and sister watched from the window. Their faces were fat with cereal, a third helping. I made a face at them when they asked how come I was working. Rick pointed to part of the lawn. "You missed some over there." I ignored him and kept my attention on the windmill of grassy blades.

While I was emptying the catcher, a bee stung the bottom of my foot. I danced on one leg and was ready to cry when Mother showed her face at the window. I sat down on the grass and examined my foot: the stinger was pulsating. I pulled it out quickly, ran water over the sting and packed it with mud, Grandmother's remedy.

Hobbling, I returned to the flower bed where I pulled more stringers and again played with the dog. More ticks had migrated to his snout. I swept the front steps, took out the garbage, cleaned the lint filter to the dryer (easy), plucked hair from the industrial wash basin in the garage (also easy), hosed off the patio, smashed three snails sucking paint from the house (disgusting but fun), tied a bundle of newspapers, put away toys, and, finally, seeing that almost everything was done and the sun was not too high, started waxing the car.

My brother joined me with an old gym sock, and our sister watched us while sucking on a cherry

Kool-Aid ice cube. The liquid wax drooled onto the sock, and we began to swirl the white slop on the chrome. My arms ached from buffing, which though less boring than weeding, was harder. But the beauty was evident. The shine, hurting our eyes and glinting like an armful of dimes, brought Mother out. She looked around the yard and said, "Pretty good." She winced at the grille and returned inside the house.

We began to wax the paint. My brother applied the liquid and I followed him rubbing hard in wide circles as we moved around the car. I began to hurry because my arms were hurting and my stung foot looked like a water balloon. We were working around the trunk when Rick pounded on the bottle of wax. He squeezed the bottle and it sneezed a few more white drops.

We looked at each other. "There's some on the sock," I said. "Let's keep going."

We polished and buffed, sweat weeping on our brows. We got scared when we noticed that the gym sock was now blue. The paint was coming off. Our sister fit ice cubes into our mouths and we worked harder, more intently, more dedicated to the car and our mother. We ran the sock over the chrome, trying to pick up extra wax. But there wasn't enough to cover the entire car. Only half got waxed, but we thought it was better than nothing and went inside for lunch. After lunch, we returned outside with tasty sandwiches.

Rick and I nearly jumped. The waxed side of the car was foggy white. We took a rag and began to polish vigorously and nearly in tears, but the fog wouldn't come off. I blamed Rick and he blamed me. Debra stood at the window, not wanting to get involved. Now, not only would we not go to the movies, but Mom would surely snap a branch from the plum tree and chase us around the yard.

Mom came out and looked at us with hands on her aproned hips. Finally, she said, "You boys worked so hard." She turned on the garden hose and washed the car. That night we did go to the drive-in. The first feature was about nothing, and the second feature, starring Jerry Lewis, was *Cinderfella*. I tried to stay awake. I kept a wad of homemade popcorn in my cheek and laughed when Jerry Lewis fit golf tees in his nose. I rubbed my watery eyes. I laughed and looked at my mom. I promised myself I would remember that scene with the golf tees and promised myself not to work so hard the coming Saturday. Twenty minutes into the movie, I fell asleep with one hand in the popcorn.

THE GROUPS

The Beatles seemed like they would wash their hands before eating, while The Rolling Stones would laugh and urinate on a wall. My best friend Scott and I liked The Stones. We sat on a canal levee, looking to the west where the sun burned a feathery blade of cloud. We were sixteen, with cut

muscles on our stomachs and one or two ideas in
our heads. One was to move out of our parents'
houses by the time we were eighteen. The other
was to be famous by twenty, and to learn to play
the guitar well enough that girls would lean out of
their Volkswagens and ask, "Are you famous?"

We weren't famous sitting on the levee. Sparrows swooped from scraggly elms to peck among
the sulfurous reeds. Toads bloated themselves on
air and hideous song, and gophers raised their fat
faces at us, Punch-and-Judy puppets come alive.

"The Animals are pretty good," Scott said. "Do
you think San Francisco is over there?"

I looked where he pointed. The blade of cloud
was gone, having either moved on or been evaporated by the Fresno sun. "Yeah, they're pretty
good." I thought of "Down in Monterey" and "Sky
Pilot," a message song about the destruction of
mankind which was now number three on the
radio. The eerie guitar and violin sounds on the
record sometimes put me in a trance and made
me think that I had lived before and was going to
live again.

Scott laughed and threw a rock at a gopher.
"Man, we used to like Freddie and the Dreamers.
Can you believe it?"

I chuckled and flapped my hands. Freddie, a
bespectacled rocker in tie and suit, had one hit,
and only because he appeared on the "Ed Sullivan
Show" flapping his arms and singing, "Do the
Freddie, Do the Freddie. Yeah, Yeah, Yeah."

"Do you think The Stones will have another
hit?" Scott asked, giving the boot to a sand spider

scurrying in the sand. It had been four months since "Ruby Tuesday," which hit number two, and eight months since "Under My Thumb," which hit number seven. Not hearing a new hit by The Stones on the radio was a cause for real concern because The Beatles were pumping them out and "Hey Jude" was on the tip of everyone's tongue. Even my mother said she liked that song, "Hey, Jew."

"Yeah," I said. "Do you think The Stones are as good as The Beatles?"

"Maybe."

"Do you think The Stones will always be together?"

"Maybe."

This scared both of us. We knew The Beatles were popular among the girls with better faces. We knew they had more hits and more movies, and they seemed smarter because you could listen to their songs and know that something was going on. The words to their songs made you want to put down your fork and just listen. And how could you dance to "Lucy in the Sky with Diamonds" ?

The canal carried dark water and a slow glimmer of sun. A sparrow waded thigh-deep in the frothy reeds along the bank. I put a heel to a sand spider and remembered someone writing somewhere that "I Am the Walrus" was about Paul, the cute Beatle, dying. It was true that no one had seen him in three months. No one had seen John, either, because Yoko was now leading him around in long fur coats.

"Do you think Paul is dead?" Scott asked.

"Maybe. But I think John is alive. He seems like a thinker." I looked west. Another cloud pulled in from out of town, whitening a portion of the sky. "Do you like Cream?"

"Not really," Scott said. "Their songs are too long. You only get three on each side."

The Beatles always had six songs to one side of their LPs. The Stones had five, which troubled me because it seemed that we Stone lovers weren't getting our money's worth. It also seemed that The Beatles had better album covers. You could stare at them in your bedroom and notice more each time.

"Do you like Led Zeppelin?" Scott asked.

Rednecks who stunk of motor oil seemed to like them, and people who ate a lot of reds and looked at dust motes for hours. "Some of their songs. But you need a good stereo for them."

Scott and I had record players with quarters taped to the arm so our scratched records wouldn't jump from their grooves. When we bought a record we always promised to keep it clean and return it to its sleeve when we finished listening. We also promised to keep it away from the Fresno sun. But after a day or two we got sloppy. One time I let my favorite Stones album warp in the sun, which had crept around the back of the house and into my bedroom. The record was warped, and no matter how many quarters I stacked on the arm of my phonograph, the needle kept jumping, like a diver on a board.

"Creedence Clearwater Revival, they're OK, huh?" I asked Scott. Scott said all their songs sounded the same, the same Okie guitar chords over and over.

Jimi Hendrix made me think of black people in a mystical way, and The Moody Blues seemed like a group with a lot to say. Simon and Garfunkel made Scott look at my bedroom wall on a rainy day and think of it as a big album cover with a heavy message. Bob Dylan seemed like he had lived his previous life as a train conductor. That was OK. Look at him now, I thought. The guy is going places.

We were going places, too, once we moved out of the house. Our stepfathers didn't like hippies. They made us cut our hair every time our scalps disappeared under a little growth of hair. They made us sing as we slaved in the yard, butchering weeds for the millionth time. Our mothers were OK. They stirred a lot of pots and steamed up their glasses from hard work. They didn't complain about dirty bedsheets or the records we played.

We wanted to move to San Francisco because the music was there, and they had clouds to block some of the heat we had known all our lives. We had it all planned. We would work as gas station attendants, something we knew about from our years of mowing lawns and filling gas cans. At night we would go to college because one of The Stones said in an interview that what he missed most of all was a college degree.

Another cargo of clouds moved in, white with the promise of snow and rain. I said something about that sissy, Donovan, and Scott remarked that The Who was getting old. I didn't have an answer for Scott about whether I thought George and Ringo were dead, too. I was too worried about The Stones not knowing how to make hits. I flicked a rock at a gopher. The sparrows pecked at their black boughs. The canal water rushed by, and we stayed put, running sand through our fingers.

THE TALK

My best friend and I knew that we were going to grow up to be ugly. On a backyard lawn—the summer light failing west of the mulberry tree where the house of the most beautiful girl on our street stood—we talked about what we could do: shake the second-base dirt from our hair, wash our hands of frog smells and canal water, and learn to smile without showing our crooked teeth. We had to stop spitting when girls were looking, and learn not to pile food onto a fork and into a fat cheek already churning hot grub.

We were twelve, with lean bodies that were beginning to grow in weird ways. First, our heads got large, but our necks wavered, frail as crisp tulips. The eyes stayed small as well, receding into pencil dots on each side of an unshapely nose that cast remarkable shadows when we turned sideways. It seemed that Scott's legs sprouted muscle and renegade veins, but his arms, blue with ink markings, stayed short and hung just below his waist. My gangly arms nearly touched my kneecaps. In this way, I was built for picking up grounders and doing cartwheels, my arms swaying just inches from the summery grass.

We sat on the lawn, with the porchlight off, waiting for the beautiful girl to turn on her bedroom light and read on her stomach with one leg stirring the air. This stirred us, and our dream was a clean dream of holding hands and airing out our loneliness by walking up and down the block.

When Scott asked who I was going to marry, I said a brown girl from the valley. He said that he was going to marry a strawberry blonde who would enjoy Millerton Lake, dirty as it was. I said mine would like cats and the sea, and would think nothing of getting up at night from a warm, restless bed and sitting in the yard under the icy stars. Scott said his wife would work for the first year or so, because he would go to trade school in refrigeration. Since our town was made with what was left over after God made hell, there was money in air conditioning, he reasoned.

I said that while my wife would clean the house and stir pots of nice grub, I would drive a truck to my job as a carpenter, which would allow me to use my long arms. I would need only a step ladder to hand a fellow worker on the roof a pinch of nails. I could hammer, saw, lift beams into place, and see the work I got done at the end of the day. Of course, she might like to work, and that would be okay, because then we could buy two cars and wave at each other if we should see the other drive by. In the evenings, we would drink Kool-Aid and throw a slipper at our feisty dog at least a hundred times before we went inside for a Pop-Tart and hot chocolate.

Scott said he would work hard too, but now and then he would find money on the street and the two of them could buy extra things like a second TV for the bedroom and a Doughboy swimming pool for his three kids. He planned on having three kids and a ranch house on the river where he could dip a hand in the water, drink, and say, "Ahh, taste good."

But that would be years later. Now we had to do something about our looks. We plucked at the grass and flung it into each other's faces.

"Rotten luck," Scott said. "My arms are too short. Look at 'em."

"Maybe we can lift weights. This would make up for our looks," I said.

"I don't think so," Scott said, depressed. "People like people with nice faces."

He was probably right. I turned onto my stomach, a stalk of grass in my mouth. "Even if I'm ugly, my wife's going to be good-looking," I said. "She'll have a lot of dresses and I'll have more shirts than I have now. Do you know how much carpenters make?"

Then I saw the bedroom light come on and the beautiful girl walk into the room drying her hair with a towel. I nudged Scott's short arm and he saw what I saw. We flicked the stalks of grass, stood up, and walked over to the fence to look at her scrub her hair dry. She plopped onto the bed and began to comb it, slowly at first because it was tangled. With a rubber band, she tied it back and picked up a book that was thick as a good-sized sandwich.

Scott and I watched her read a book, now both legs in the air and twined together, her painted toenails like red petals. She turned the pages slowly, very carefully, and now and then lowered her face into the pillow. She looked sad but beautiful, and we didn't know what to do except nudge each other in the heart and creep away to the front yard.

"I can't stand it anymore. We have to talk about this," Scott said.

"If I try, I think I can make myself better looking," I said. "I read an article about a girl whitening her teeth with water and flour."

So we walked up the street, depressed. For every step I took, Scott took two, his short arms pumping to keep up. For every time Scott said, "I think we're ugly," I said two times, "Yeah, yeah, we're in big trouble."

THE COMPUTER DATE

At sixteen, neither Scott nor I was religious. We spent most of our time sitting on a levee pouring sand through our hands and looking west. That was the way our older friends went. They boarded buses and got the hell out, a fissure of light follow-

ing them down highway 99 to 152. The next time
we saw them, tattoos ran up and down their arms.
They were in the army. Their voices were deep as
a sack full of frogs, and the first worry lines cut
across their brow.

In high school, girls were blossoms shaken from
a tree and blooming with life. We didn't know how
to talk to them, so we rehearsed by the school
fountain. "Do you go to this school?" Scott asked,
and I punched him in the arm. "Of course they do.
Why else would they be here?"

I tried, "I walked by your house and saw that
you have a palm tree. I have a palm tree. What a
coincidence."

Scott tried: "It's cold for December."

I tried: "A June bug can live on a screen door for
days."

Scott tried: "It rains a lot in April, but the funny
thing is the rain is either very cold or very warm
but never in between."

I tried: "My friend Tony said he would take the
bullet for the president."

Scott tried: "Chicken is my favorite food."

We needed help. When Scott's sister said we
should go to her Christian youth group because
young people were being matched by computer,
we bathed with Lava, a pumice-like bar of soap,
and wore the nicest ironed shirts from our closets.
We walked downtown, neither of us talking much
because, we thought, talking stunk up a guy's
breath, especially if the subject was girls. We
looked around a lot, nervous and perspiring faint

moons from our underarms. But we were happy to finally get a chance to find a girlfriend.

The youth group rented the Fresno Convention Center. We were greeted by some very happy college students in red jackets who went around shaking everyone's hands. They shook mine, and I got sort of sick because their hands were moist. What I remembered most of my Catholic school education was that Sister Marie had said, "Evil dwells in moist places."

I let the thought go. After the five-mile walk, we were glad for the cool air. We found seats. I was amazed at how many teenagers filled the auditorium. It was the most ironed shirts and dresses I had ever seen.

When the lights dimmed, everyone found a seat and became quiet. A well-dressed man, the minister, appeared in the spotlight. His head was bowed, and when I looked around I noticed that everyone's head was bowed. He said a prayer, each phrase sounding like the end of something very sad and final. Then a youngish man appeared with his guitar and sang Christian songs. The first guy returned and spoke on the subject of invisible faith. He seemed pretty serious, and I thought that at any moment he was going to cry and embarrass the crowd.

Toward the end of the evening, the happy college students who greeted us at the door came out on the stage. They were still happy. They held up computer cards and fanned them like decks of playing cards. The teenagers in the bleachers nearly stampeded for them, and would have except we had to say more prayers about good, clean fun. Then the cards were distributed.

I was anxious. While the minister said prayers, Scott and I walked up and down the aisles looking at the girls. Some were attractive, and some were OK. Only a few were really ugly. We also noticed that there were more girls than boys, and that most of the boys wore crooked glasses on the ends of their noses. We snapped our fingers and said, "What luck!"

We licked our pencils and answered questions like: What is your nationality? What is your goal in life? How often do you go to church? How much do you weigh? Who is your favorite actor/actress? What is your favorite food?

The food question was easy for Scott, but I spent a lot of time worrying about how to spell spaghetti since the red pencils didn't have erasers. Instead of risking poor spelling, I wrote in capitals, MEAT-BALLS.

We sang more songs, then hurried away without shaking anyone's hand. On the way home, we talked up a storm because we didn't have to worry about spoiling our breath. We didn't have to worry about perspiring either, or about accounting for our time because we had had good, clean fun.

The next day Scott and I sat near the fountain and argued over the nationality question. Scott had written, "White." I argued, "That ain't a nationality." He said nearly a hundred times that it was and that I was jealous because there were no more than nine Mexican girls at the Christian youth group convention and three were too large to fit in a car. We got in a fight and stayed away from each other for two days.

But by the weekend we were friends once more. We decided not to return to find out who we were matched with. Instead, we drove to the levee, where we watched a horn of moon hang over the canal water. We were more lonely than ever. We talked and talked because it didn't matter if our breath stank. I showed Scott where my first tattoo would go—a panther on my bicep, and he showed me the place on his chest where a naked lady would stand. We drove back to town and spent the rest of the evening revving the car up to sixty on quiet streets and braking as hard as we could without our faces going through the windshield. The evening, bad as it was, was not worth dying for.

THE WRESTLERS

It hurt to be pinned in twelve seconds in a non-league wrestling match, especially at the end of the 1960s when, except for a few dads and moms and the three regulars with faces like punched-in paper bags, the bleachers were empty of spectators. It hurt to stand under the shower looking at fingerprints still pressed in my arm where my opponent, whose name was Bloodworth, gripped, yanked, and with a grin on his face threw me on my back. The guy next to me had fingerprints around his wrists and arm. Another guy was red around his chest. His eyes were also red. We lost by plenty that night, but coach wasn't too mad. He beat his clipboard against his khaki thigh and joked, "You were a bunch of fishes," by which he meant that we were an easy catch. He pretended to be upset, but we knew that it was the beginning of the season and there was still hope.

I showered and dressed. My best friend Scott was waiting in his Ford Galaxy. He was throwing corn nuts into his mouth, churning beautifully on the taste of salt and roasted nuts. I told him that corn nuts were not good for him, and he asked how that could be, because they tasted good. That night we drove around for a while before he dropped me off at my house and asked me for a quarter. Gas don't come free, he said. It costs money when you lose before you get started.

I wrestled that year and needed to be driven around because I could manage only three feeble wins against nine losses. Driving around Fresno was therapy. We took the corners sharply and felt the give of Pep-Boy shocks, which for me was the most exciting discovery since our biology teacher made a pretty girl kiss a petri dish and three days later, fungus climbed over the sides. We cornered so that the tires squealed and the inertia pulled our saliva from one side of our mouths to the other. I liked that feeling, liked how Scott would be talking about an episode of *Bonanza* or *Gunsmoke* and suddenly brake hard so that we had to brace ourselves against the dash. Sometimes it hurt, and sometimes if felt just wonderful to lift from the seat and almost smash into the glass.

I had taken driver's ed from my coach, and on the second day of class he said, "Don't be scared but you're gonna see some punks getting killed." The film was called something like "Red Asphalt" or "Blood on the Pavement," but I remember a narrator with a crew cut and a neck as thick as a canned ham. When he spoke while holding up a tennis shoe, the muscles in his neck jumped around. He said, "The boy who wore this sneaker is dead." He held it up, and the camera moved in close on the high-top, then flashed to a freeway accident as dramatic music started along with the title credits.

It could have been my sneaker because, like the dead kid, I liked high-tops. It could have been Scott's or any other boy's. The film was meant to scare us, but most of the boys enjoyed it. The girls looked away when the film showed six seconds of a car wreck from different angles. The sound of metal and glass breaking made us listen up. It stopped us from chewing our gum or slipping a corn nut into the inside of our cheeks. Then all was quiet. A bird pumped his tail and chirped on a chain link fence. The narrator came back on. He was standing on the shoulder of a freeway, his tie whipping in the wind of traffic. He warned us that during a head-on collision, your clothes rip off: shirts, skirts, shoes, the whole works—naked as you were born, only you were dead.

I recalled Bloodworth pinning me in twelve seconds and suddenly realized life was getting shorter: a car wreck could kill you in six seconds. It was tough luck—only half the time for the kids in the film. I watched the film, then watched coach laugh along with the boys and turn on the overhead lights, jumble the dimes and quarters in his deep pockets, and slap his clipboard against his thigh. His neck was thick like the narrator's. His hair was a little longer and shiny as the black industrial shoes on his feet. Right in drivers ed, among the idiot boys smelling of sunflower seeds and corn nuts, I realized that wrestlers went on to do more than slam people into mats.

I was a junior that year. During my senior year I was so lonely that I needed to drive around Fresno. Scott was at the wheel, more lonely than me, more desperate because a girl said no, then yes, then finally no again to a Halloween date. It was no for both of us. We had no choice but to drive around corners, the centrifugal force pulling us one way, then another. We had no choice but to throw bottles from the car and sneer at old drivers in long cars.

We often parked at the levee and looked at the water. I said things like, "Scott, I think I've lived before," or, "Scotty, do you ever feel that someone is gripping your shoulder and when you turn around, no one is there? It's spooky." I could still feel Bloodworth's grip on my arm, and would feel it for years.

I didn't like high school. Coach knew only so many words. The dean's hand trembled when he touched door knobs. Our teacher kept repeating that a noun was a person, place or thing. She stood at the blackboard, lipstick overrunning her mouth, and said for the thousandth time: Elvis is a noun. Fresno is a noun. Elvis's guitar is also a noun.

The water in the canal was quick as a wind-blown cloud. The 1960s were coming to an end, and the first of the great rock stars were beginning to die. We were dying to leave home, by car, thumb or on water racing west to where the sun went down.

THE RIVER

Scott and I traveled by Greyhound up highway 99 with its splattered dogs and wind-hurt olean-ders, through valley towns stinking of gasoline and rage, and up the Tehachapi, which from far away was purple with shadow but up close was yellow from the death of tiny flowers. We traveled six hours to Los Angeles, walked four miles, and leaned from 7:30 to 9:30 on someone's Dodge Dart in Hollywood. Rod Stewart and The Faces was playing, and although we didn't have the six dollars to get into the Palladium, we liked the thought of being close to a band that was so loud it was great.

Because we were seventeen, something had to happen. There were mobs of young people in leather vests, bell-bottoms, beads, Jesus thongs, tie-dyed T-shirts, and crowns of flowers. Almost all

of them had long hair that smelled of cigarettes
and burgers. We were surrounded by patchouli oil,
sweat, Red Mountain wine, incense, and a lot of
beautiful screwing, we supposed. We leaned
against the fender of the Dodge, which was like
my stepfather's car, only the trunk was pleated
from being hit. I thought of giving a peace sign to
some hippy-looking guys, but I felt too foolish, too
out of it because my pant legs were too straight
and my wrestler's haircut showed blue knots on
my head. We risked sitting on the fender, though,
and tapped a beat on our thighs. We rocked our
heads when we heard a car radio. We smiled at
three girls, but they looked straight ahead as they
walked by holding sticks of incense.

We had a lot of fun just looking. I was so happy
that I bought a bootleg LP of The Faces with only
four songs and a poorly printed cover with the
word "Live." Scott was happy, too. He bought a
burger with a Coke that was mostly ice. The two of
us sucked on toothpicks as we walked around feeling less embarrassed about giving the peace sign.
When we asked for directions to Maywood, where
my Uncle Shorty the foundry worker lived, a guy
with a roach-clip earring said it was farther than
we could walk. He pointed to the corner and said
if we stood there a car would pick us up and drive
us part of the way.

It was true. We were picked up and after a crazy
freeway drive we were let off at the Slauson exit.
Only after the car sped away, its one working tail-
light blinking as the car turned recklessly back

onto the freeway, did we think that we were finally learning how to live without worry.

The street was a four-lane river of black asphalt hardened by junky cars and diesels. Steam rose from a manhole cover. Glass sounded under our shoes. The one gas station was either closed or abandoned. We knew this place, but from where? We brought out our map, and Scott's dirty finger, then my dirty finger, crawled around the streets until we found Slauson, then Atlantic Blvd., which my uncle, who at that moment was getting off the night shift, told us to look for. We started walking west, up Slauson, and in less than a mile the place was so dark that a few stars came alive above the occasional streetlight.

We walked three miles, covering block after ugly block stinking of machinery and oil. Our loneliness was as deep as oil. Scott said that by next year he would be in the army. I said I'd be there with him, and the only thing that could kill us in Vietnam was a bayonet. We would live a long time. We could hide behind trees. Shrapnel had only one way to go and that was up, and the way we were going to fight was to hug the ground and shoot only when others told us to shoot.

We talked about not dying. Few cars traveled up the street, and when they did, we ducked behind one thing or another. Our breathing quickened and we felt excited at the fact that we could hide in such a large city. That's how it would be in the war, we told ourselves, and wondered if our eyes reflected light, like a cat's. We talked about our eyes and family until we came to a canal that nearly stopped our breathing. It was wide but dry, nothing like the canal back home. While ours was made of sand, reeds, and feeble fish stunted by the chemicals from agricultural runoff, this canal was made of mangled bicycles, tires, chairs, pissy little puddles, and winos washed downstream to settle on rafts of cardboard.

But it was no canal. Under an orange streetlight, our map said it was the Los Angeles River. We leaned over the side and spit into that fishless, waterless river. We were learning. Scott said that he knew for sure that we would live a long time. I said that I couldn't believe I was seventeen. We spit some more and looked at the skyline of power lines and industry. Turning away, we walked over the viaduct, our shoes ringing on the cement, and this time we didn't duck when a car passed, its sweep of headlights glittering the richness of shattered glass.

We made a bed of two blankets on my uncle's floor that night. Some white light from a twenty-four-hour Safeway came into the front window. I thought of Braly Street and family, some of whom were now dead, and how when Uncle returned from the Korean War, he slept on a cot on the sunporch. We had only the floor. We had yet to go and come back from our war and find ourselves a life other than the one we were losing.